Teaching Writing Across the Curriculum

FOURTH EDITION

PRENTICE HALL RESOURCES FOR WRITING

Art Young

Clemson University

PEARSON

Prentice Hall

Upper Saddle River, New Jersey 07458

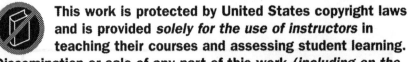

Copyright © 2006 by Pearson Education, Inc.
Upper Saddle River, New Jersey 07458
All rights reserved

Printed in the United States of America
10 9 8 7 6 5 4 3 2 1

ISBN 0-13-193664-6

◼ Table of Contents

With love, for

Donna, Molly, Sarah, Kelsey, Patricia, Rosemary, and Rose

■ Acknowledgements

Throughout this book, I quote or refer to numerous colleagues and students, most of whom are from the two universities where I have been a professor, Michigan Technological University and Clemson University. Without their talent, insight, and collaboration, this book would not be possible, and I thank them all. In the preparation of this 4th edition, I particularly want to acknowledge my wife and colleague, Donna Reiss, for her wisdom and her incomparable writing and editing skills, and for her love, encouragement, patience, and good humor. Liz Wright, a graduate research assistant in the Master of Professional Communication degree program at Clemson University, has been a knowledgeable guide and editor throughout this project, and I will be forever grateful for her able assistance in all my recent work in teaching, research, and program administration. Four people who served as mentors as well as colleagues and friends during my career—William Powers, Toby Fulwiler, Dixie Goswami, and Carl Lovitt—and each of them have influenced whatever are the best parts of this book. I take responsibility for those parts that do not measure up to their high standards of substance and style. I express my gratitude to colleagues with whom I have worked closely in the past couple of years and who have furthered my thinking in myriads of ways about writing across the curriculum and communication across the curriculum: Andy Billings, Patti Connor-Greene, Teddi Fishman, Katie Fischer, Morgan Gresham, Magnus Gustafsson, Angie Justice, Catherine Mobley, Jan Murdoch, Michael Neal, Catherine Paul, Barbara Ramirez, Nancy Swanson, Summer Taylor, Jerry Waldvogel, and Kathi Yancey. Special thanks also to all the teachers who participate in Clemson's "poetry across the curriculum" and "creative response for learning" projects, both initiatives of our communication-across-the-curriculum program. And for suggesting that I write a 4th edition of *Teaching Writing Across the Curriculum* and providing the necessary encouragement, I thank Paul Crockett of Prentice-Hall.

■Chapter 1: Introduction

Purpose

This book is written for college teachers in all disciplines. It provides a brief introduction to writing across the curriculum (WAC), its theory and its practice, with the emphasis on practice—on teaching, on using writing as *a tool for learning* the subject being studied, and as a strategy for improving the confidence and the ability of students to communicate effectively. This booklet should serve as a guide to teachers who have been assigned, or who have volunteered, to teach a required "writing-intensive" course in their discipline as well as to faculty who decide to include student writing, whether occasionally or frequently, in their courses. Although my primary audience is faculty members in all disciplines, I expect this booklet to be useful to writing program directors in English departments who often coordinate writing-across-the-curriculum programs or who are responsible for integrating writing across the curriculum with a required first-year composition course. Also, I hope it will be useful to teachers-in-training and to graduate teaching assistants in all disciplines.

History

Although writing in college courses is certainly not a novel idea, I associate its recent incarnation in WAC with the "language for learning" movement in England in the 1960s and 1970s under the leadership of James Britton, Nancy Martin, and their colleagues in the School Council Project. The focus in England was on writing in the schools, but when the concept moved across the Atlantic in the mid 1970s, it made its initial landings at the college level. By the mid-1980s, a national survey conducted by the Modern Language Association found that one-third of U.S. colleges and universities had a WAC program. Over the past thirty years, WAC has continued to grow on the nation's college campuses, and it has become a viable factor for educational reform in the nation's schools.

My own involvement with WAC began in 1976 at the end of spring term, when a biology professor telephoned me, a new English department head, to find out how a senior in medical technology could write a "semi-literate" report for him after receiving a grade of B from me in a first-year composition course. My first reaction, as you might expect, was defensive. Was he implying that I couldn't recognize "semi-literacy," that I had no standards for effective expression, that grade inflation had gotten the best of me, or, worse, that I was an incompetent teacher? Once I determined that his question was an honest one, that his anger—and he was angry—was not directed at me alone, but rather at a system of education that allowed such things to happen, we decided to meet together, and with the student, to see what we could learn about this thorny situation. How could a graduating senior from a selective university with a 3.3 grade point average be "semi-literate"?

What we discovered may not seem surprising today, but it surprised me at the time. As I read the student's report, I had to agree that it was unacceptable for a senior, soon-to-be a college graduate. And yet, the student, Mary, was an

1

A-B student in most of the courses she had taken over the previous four years. So what went wrong?

Attitudes and Expectations

Here are just some of the things we learned as we talked with Mary. She didn't understand the nature and expectations of the assignment; she assumed because this was a biology course and not an English course, concerns for a focused introduction, purposeful organization, and attention to spelling and punctuation would not matter. If she had understood that they do matter (the biology professor assumed that seniors understood this and that he would not have to reiterate these basics of good writing), she could have delivered a much more effective report. And indeed she did, when offered the opportunity to revise. So, in this case, Mary knew how to perform the basics, she just didn't think scientists "cared about this stuff." How had she developed such an attitude? As we talked with her further, we discovered that she had not really written anything more than one or two pages long since her first-year English course and that she had never written a substantial scientific report until this professor's class. So during her last semester at college, Mary was doing the first significant piece of writing in her discipline.

It so happens that during this same period of time, our university was considering ways to improve the communication abilities of all our students. Several factors had led us to this point: national publicity about a literacy crisis ("Why Johnny can't read or write"), the advent of the "information society," complaints from employers about our graduates ("technically very competent, but weak on communication skills"), and a growing recognition that communication was an increasingly important and demanding aspect of work in and out of the academy.

The episode with Mary focused on several key issues for us. One change we considered was adding a required junior-level course in writing, taught by the English department, for all students; we realized, however, that Mary would pass such a course as easily as she had passed my first-year course but would continue to see writing courses as a hurdle, as something extraneous to her professional education, would continue to see sustained writing as something one does in English courses but not science courses, and would continue to do little writing in her major courses since her teachers could assume that others on the campus would take care of her writing needs. After all, hadn't the university just added yet another required writing course?

Another change we considered was adding a junior-level proficiency exam and requiring students to take remedial courses until they passed it. But we realized that our biology student would easily pass such a test and yet never experience her writing as an integral component of her professional education. And again, when she passed the test, we would be sending a message to the rest of the faculty that she was a proficient writer in all subjects in all contexts. We were beginning to realize that part of learning to be a biologist was learning to write like a biologist and that to be able to write like a biologist one needed to know what a biologist knows and what a biologist knows how to do. We came to believe that writing was integral to a professional education in biology (and

2

every other discipline) and not simply a generic skill easily mastered in one or two courses and then transferred effortlessly to all disciplines.

Teaching and Learning

Just as this emblematic experience with the biology student kept us from making some costly mistakes, it also pointed us in a new direction: writing across the curriculum. A simple definition of WAC is that students use written language to develop and communicate knowledge in every discipline and across disciplines. In practice, it often assumes an interdisciplinary effort in which teachers from different disciplines work together to develop a comprehensive program that might include coordination among first-year composition courses, general education courses, writing-intensive courses in the major, and senior capstone courses. But the focus of early WAC programs was—and my focus here is—on teaching and learning and not on curriculum and assessment. To be sure, curriculum and assessment are important components of a comprehensive writing program, but WAC begins with teachers and students learning together through written language. To begin with curriculum and assessment would be to repeat the mistake we almost made in 1976 when we thought of adding a required writing course and an exit exam as a way of improving students' communication abilities, rather than beginning with teachers. WAC assumes that teachers, not curriculum and assessment, are the center of the educational process and the key to educational reform.

The Workshop Approach

Thus, in 1978, we began a series of interdisciplinary faculty workshops, designed by Toby Fulwiler and other colleagues, as highly interactive sessions in which faculty shared the problems and the possibilities of writing in their disciplines and generated new and more effective ways to incorporate writing in their courses. Those first workshops lasted from two to four days, and each one was attended by about twenty-five faculty. Since that time, similar workshop models, with modifications to fit local situations, have been held on hundreds of college campuses across the nation. This booklet stems from my experience conducting such workshops. It's based on the knowledge I've gained from colleagues in nearly every discipline—accounting and zoology, English and communication studies, engineering and forestry. And it's based on the convenient way I've learned to organize these workshops into two interrelated parts: writing to learn and writing to communicate. I recognize that this division is arbitrary—that communication goes on in writing to learn and that learning goes on in the struggle to communicate, but I've found that this distinction often enables teachers to generate new perspectives and strategies in their teaching. I also recognize that to talk about teaching and learning in a generic way is fraught with difficulties, because teaching and learning changes in each situation—when we consider what is being taught, by whom, to whom, for what reasons, and under what conditions. I've attempted to provide examples from a variety of sources so that teachers in widely differing situations might be able to relate and adapt my suggestions to their own situations. I've constructed this booklet, then, along the line of the workshops I conduct, with plenty of student

3

examples from different levels and disciplines and with discussions and suggestions provided by the numerous faculty and student colleagues at Michigan Technological University, Clemson University, and elsewhere with whom I've shared a workshop, a lunch, a class, or a piece of writing. I am grateful to them all.

■ Chapter 2: Writing To Learn

Many readers will expect that the first item of business in this section will be a definition of "writing to learn." What exactly is it, anyway? I ask such readers to be patient but also to be active participants in this inductive learning process—one in which we'll build definitions through examples and experiences. Proceeding in this way, I hope that whatever knowledge is gained will come with an understanding of implications and limitations. Although I will offer numerous practical suggestions for teaching with writing, I want to forgo the temptation to say "Do this on Monday morning: it's a can't-miss technique," as if good teaching is simply a listing of successful techniques and assignments. Rather, successful assignments are embedded in the unique goals of each course and are integral to the building of knowledge in that course. Effective writing assignments are not "add-ons" to fulfill a writing requirement or to generate 20 percent of a final grade.

"My Utopia": An Example

Let us begin, as I often begin a faculty workshop, by reading together a piece of student writing. Here is some context for the writing that follows. On the first day of class, a philosophy professor meets the forty students in his Introduction to Philosophy course. The students are mostly engineering majors fulfilling a humanities elective. He goes over the syllabus and course goals and explains that the first unit of the course will be on the subject of utopias. During the next month, the class will read Thomas More's *Utopia* and B. F. Skinner's *Walden Two* as well as some relevant essays. Teacher and students discuss briefly their initial concept of utopia, and then as the class ends, the teacher assigns the first piece of writing: "As a way of getting us started, please write a brief essay on what your utopia, as you conceive of it right now, looks like. What are some of its features? Now this writing should have a quick turnaround time, so it is due Wednesday, our next class meeting. I would like you to spend about a half hour or so writing it—just about three hundred words—no library research needed— just your own ideas—get them down on paper—for me and your classmates to read."

On Wednesday, most students bring their writing to class, one or two handwritten pages. Before we read the one written by Thomas, please reflect on the three prompts I ask workshop participants to consider in a brief written response (in their workshop notebooks).

1. Give your reaction to this student's writing: what you found interesting, surprising, troublesome, and also strengths and weaknesses.

2. Consider how you might use such student writing in your classroom.

3. Consider how you would respond to this student.

Here is the essay submitted by Thomas:

My Utopia

From my point of view the perfect society would be a small community nestled in the mountains—away from the masses of people and cities. There would be small businesses, but mainly crafts would be the large portion of employment. It would be a closed society in the sence that any one who didn't live there could not come in and find employment. Therefore only enough people could live there that there was jobs available for and there were only enough jobs to support about 5,000.

The economic nature would be as follows: All jobs would have a fixed salary the only way to get increased wages would be to move up in position or status. There would be no inflation because all prices would be fixed. There wouldn't be room for competition because there would only be one firm or one shop for each craft. With no unemployment or inflation people would never have to worry about a decrease in their standard of living. Everyone can still be in whatever class they want, as far as lower, upper or middle classes, as long as they are productive members of society. You must want to earn a living in order to live here. There are no taxes: no welfare programs—the incomes received would allow them to purchase anything they want and they would be able to work as long as they want, age wise.

The government would be composed of a few people who would act more like a committee than a pres., vice pres., partlimentary group. There purpose is to see that the fixed prices were followed and act kind of like a supreme court. The only rules would be the 10 commandments and if any of these are broken, this is cause enough to expel them from the society.

Faculty participants read and reflect on "My Utopia," and then we hold a brainstorming session in which differing perspectives are encouraged and in which criticism of one another's initial reactions is not allowed. Some of the most frequent reactions to the first prompt include the following:

This student is so illiterate, he should not be in college.

I wish half my students could write so well.

I'm put off by all the errors in spelling, grammar, and punctuation.

It is well organized, with a beginning, middle, and end.

His utopia sounds appealing—back to nature—like Thoreau.

His utopia sounds totalitarian, worse than communism.

He honestly gives his first reaction as the assignment asks.

Poor logic and confusion in thinking: who would choose to be in the lower class? No "room for competition," but you can still "move up"?

Lots of questions need to be answered and issues clarified: How would people (over 5000) be kept out? Would there be any children left if one disobedient act got them expelled? Is he saying people can stop work at age 22? People can have low wages yet buy anything they want? What will they be able to buy besides "crafts"?

His utopia has many good features of concern to many people: job security with a good standard of living, a safe law and order society, apparent equality and mutual respect among citizens, an escape from the complexity of contemporary living.

I'm surprised at how well he did in a half hour on a subject he hadn't studied before.

After we generate a long list of initial reactions, we do not try to reach consensus or a resolution. Rather we move into a brainstorming session of prompt number 2. What ways might Thomas's and others' writing be used in the course? Frequent responses include the following:

To get class discussion going about the characteristics of utopia.

As a basis for brainstorming: with teacher or a classmate listing characteristics on the board.

Use Thomas's writing (anonymously) as an example of bad writing.

Use this writing as the first in a sequence of informal writings designed to build on the students' increasing knowledge.

Ask selected students to read theirs to the class.

Ask students to read to each other in groups of four or five—so that they can get new ideas or change ideas about their fledgling utopias.

Ask students to read and critique each other's writing in pairs.

Ask students to put their writing away for a month and then to take it out and reflect on how their utopias have changed as they have learned more; or, after a month, ask Thomas and the others to critique the logic of their earlier writing.

Ask students to compare the main point in their utopias with those of Thomas More and B. F. Skinner.

Ask students to revise these beginning reflections into a formal essay after they have studied and discussed more about utopias.

At the end of the unit, ask students to write a formal essay on utopia—the audience for this essay will be the naïve writers of the first day.

And then workshop participants move on to discuss the second part of prompt number 3—how they would respond to Thomas:

Mark all the errors on his paper but don't give it a grade.

Mark only the most important errors at this stage.

Send Thomas to the campus writing center for remedial help.

Only write interactive questions in the margins that will encourage further thought: "Why do you want to avoid competition in your utopia?"

Only write encouraging comments to motivate students to read, write, and learn more.

No written response at all—just read them and refer to them during the next lecture or discussion.

No need to collect it and respond: ask students to save writing in a portfolio for further use as the course progresses.

There is usually some tension in the air by this time in the workshop. Some teachers believe that if you only put encouraging remarks on Thomas's paper (or no remarks at all) you are misleading him into believing that his writing and thinking are satisfactory; others believe that if you mark every error and fault in logic on his first paper, he may feel overwhelmed, discouraged, betrayed, and less motivated to contribute, to take risks, and to share his thoughts. Most seem to agree that the value of the assignment, if there is value, is not as training in formal writing (except perhaps as notes toward a formal draft) but rather as an icebreaker to motivate students to be active learners and class participants, to aid the teacher in getting to know the class and enhance student-teacher communication, to help the students discover what they already know about utopias as well as what they have to learn, to build a sense of community among students undertaking a joint enterprise, to increase students' interest in this academic subject by relating it to their lives and values, to build a personal and academic context for further reading and writing about utopias. And yet questions remain: Should students be required to write about something they know little about, to write what are sure to be unformed and uninformed ideas, to share the results with classmates and teacher? Shouldn't writing assignments on "utopia" wait until the students have read primary and secondary sources, listened to lectures, asked questions of the teacher, know something worth writing about?

Writing To Learn and Writing To Communicate

One way to think about the classroom uses of writing is to consider writing as a valuable tool for learning as well as for communication. If we are willing to consider making such a distinction, then we can talk about designing certain writing assignments primarily to help students learn the material of the course and other assignments to help them communicate what they have learned to others. These two purposes for assignments, which are not mutually exclusive, then guide us in two distinct ways to read and respond to student writing based on the different roles most teachers play: teacher as mentor and teacher as judge. Here is a chart that may make this distinction clearer.

Writing and Thinking

↙   ↘

Writing To Learn   **Writing To Communicate**

- Discovery thinking

- Invention: uttered, generated

- Writer-based prose
  (explains matter to oneself)

- Audience: self and
  trusted others

- Personal language
  in social community

- Teacher as facilitator

- Personal knowledge

- Forms: journals, field notes,
  rough drafts, blogs

- Critical thinking

- Revision: crafted, clarified

- Reader-based prose
  (explains matter to others)

- Audience: distant

- Formal language
  of discourse community

- Teacher as professional

- Contextual knowledge

- Forms: essays, reports,
  business letters, web publications

↘   ↙

Discovery
and
Critical Understanding

Look first at the left column of my "Writing and Thinking" chart. The promulgation and practice of "writing to learn" throughout the curriculum is one of the major contributions of the WAC movement. When a teacher designs a writing-to-learn assignment, such as "My Utopia," he or she offers, as James Britton has said, an opportunity "to explain the matter to oneself," when the "matter" can be net ionic equations in chemistry or the Battle of Gettysburg in history. A writing-to-communicate assignment, on the other hand, challenges the student "to explain the matter to others." Following Britton's reasoning, we can understand the difficulty, if not the impossibility, of explaining the matter to others before you have explained it to yourself. And because writing to learn has traditionally been underutilized in instruction, the WAC movement encourages adding writing to learn to most courses for two principal purposes: (1) students will learn the material better and (2) this better understanding will lead to improved written communication.

I return to the left column of the "Writing and Thinking" chart to annotate it briefly:

- *Discovery thinking:* Writing to learn is associated with discovery writing and drafting—Thomas discovering (provisionally, of course) what his utopia might look like.

- *Invention: uttered, generated:* An early part of the writing process—make words and ideas visible so they can be examined, played with, or discarded.

- *Writer-based prose:* Writing that usually makes sense to the writer—who is close to the language and the context—but that may not hold much meaning for others.

- *Audience: self and trusted others:* Writing that may never be shown to others, as when a physicist keeps a private journal of speculations and imaginings, or that may be shown to others who can be trusted to be supportive readers—such as a teacher in the role of trusted mentor, or a reader who expects to see mistakes and incompleteness as part of the learning process (in writing, in mechanical engineering, in everything else) but who reads looking for fresh ideas and new insights in order to encourage further learning.

- *Personal language in social community:* This is the language that writers have easiest access to for thinking—the language students own as they enter our classes—this is a powerful language for learning, and teachers as mentors should allow students access to it (as opposed to insisting on formal academic language in writing-to-learn assignments).

- *Creative:* I associate writing to learn with right-brain activity and creative problem solving.

- *Personal integration of knowledge:* Writing to learn assists in integrating new knowledge into a writer's existing system of knowledge and beliefs—a major component of "explaining the matter to oneself."

- *Forms: journals, field notes, rough drafts, blogs:* And I might add freewrites, fastwrites, one-minute essays, and other informal writings designed to encourage personal reflection and active engagement in learning, such as "My Utopia."

Writing to learn privileges the learner's language and values. Writing to communicate privileges the reader's language and values. The primary goal of writing to learn is *to please the writer* by leading to new discoveries, information, and perspectives. The primary goal of writing to communicate is *to please the reader* in providing new discoveries, information, and perspectives. This may be a single reader, as when an employee writes a memo to a supervisor, or it may be a community of readers, as when a psychology researcher writes an article for a specialized journal in behavioral science. In each case, the writer wants to be heard and taken seriously, and the shift in purpose and audience from writing to learn makes additional demands on the writer. Although I will discuss writing to communicate later in the book (47-68), let me annotate the right side of my chart for comparison's sake.

- *Critical thinking:* Writing to communicate is associated with the self-conscious arranging, manipulating, and presenting of words and ideas for some rhetorical purpose (to inform a reader, to persuade a reader).

- *Revision: crafted, clarified:* A later stage of the writing process—sentences, ideas, thinking are clarified by being reworked.

- *Reader-based prose:* Readers want to process information effectively and efficiently, and thus writers attempt to conform to reader expectations on such things as structure and conventions.

- *Audience: distant:* The writer is not close to readers, who are often judgmental, so the writer must earn their reading time—teachers read student writing critically as mentors encouraging revision, and they read student writing in their role as evaluators for how well it meets readers' expectations.

- *Formal language of discourse community:* Writers enter and write the language of a community or communities—as writers move from being students of geology to becoming geologists they learn the discourse conventions of writing and thinking as geologists do.

- *Analytic:* I associate writing to communicate with left-brain activity and systematic problem solving.

- *Objective understanding of knowledge:* Writing to communicate often means integrating the writer's information or perspective into a reader's existing system of knowledge and beliefs—as when an astronomer reports the discovery of a new star to other astronomers.

- *Forms: essays, reports, business letters, web publications:* And other forms designed to enhance the transfer of information from writers to readers.

At the conclusion of my "Writing and Thinking" chart, I relate writing to learn and writing to communicate to both discovery and critical understanding because I realize that these processes are interrelated and overlapping. Certainly writers discover new ideas in the act of revision and use their creativity in performing analytic tasks. My dualistic chart is not meant to be a theoretical construct as much as a heuristic for thinking about different ways to help students write to learn and learn to write.

I also use this chart as a framework for looking at student writing in new and productive ways. For example, Thomas in "My Utopia" has been given a write-to-learn assignment, and he has responded appropriately by taking a half-hour to jot down some initial thoughts without paying too much attention to such things as logical coherence or editing. I believe that teachers who give such assignments should recognize that they generate fairly impromptu personal reflections in writer-based prose and therefore should respond to them in the teacher-as-mentor role, not worrying about spelling errors (in this kind of writing) but only about what kinds of responses will encourage further learning. Conflict arises when the teacher assigns writing to learn and then the teacher (or other readers) reads it as writing to communicate—as a thoughtful, crafted, final product. This is undoubtedly what happens when some faculty at workshops see Thomas's writing as unsatisfactory in almost every way. On the other hand, Mary's senior biology report offers an example of poor communication between teacher and student. Mary naively thought that her biology professor would accept a discovery draft of her scientific report as a successful final product. She had never turned in such a lengthy report to him or any other biology professor. Her report rambled from point to point in no logical order, and she was not attentive to reader-based needs. The professor had assigned a write-to-communicate assignment, and he read with professional expectations that surprised Mary, but once she was made aware of them she was able to write a report that better satisfied the reader's needs. If James Britton is correct, then students who write discovery drafts are engaging in a productive exercise that ought to be encouraged—they are getting their ideas down so they can better craft them and understand them. But they should understand that discovery drafts are usually unsatisfactory as final drafts of writing that must conform to reasonable reader-based needs. Teachers can help students in a variety of ways to understand the processes by which scholars and researchers generate and communicate knowledge by distinguishing between these two kinds of writing, both of which are necessary and valuable to most of us.

The Example of Thomas Edison

Inventor and entrepreneur Thomas Edison was a prolific writer. Most workshop participants are surprised to learn that five and a half million pages of his surviving laboratory notebooks and other papers are currently being studied by scholars. Edison is well known to most of us as a famous "hands-on" engineer, working long hours in his laboratory, but we don't usually think of him as a "writer." And while he did not often write for publication, he wrote hundreds of pocket-size notebook pages per week. These notebooks are filled with speculations, plans, critiques, rough technical drawings, thinking on paper, visualizing on paper. They are written in writer-based prose to Edison himself as audience or sometimes to his colleagues in his laboratories. Here is a brief section from an entry in his Greenwich Cable Telegraph Pocket Notebook of June 10, 1873:

> ascertain if some magnetic arrangement might not be made so as to be included with the circuit to wor so that it would exactly neutralize the static charge in So many knots of Cable if these devices Could be put in the Cable & their Capacity would remain as Constant as the Capacity of the Cable = it would be valuable =
>
> Try two insulated disks of rubber on which is a strip of Zinc & of Copper Connected together= This stands still now another disk 100th of an inch from it revolves slowly & also with immense rapidity This disk has one Strip Copper. See if influence would generate E. & Connect to Sensitive Galvanometer= (*The Papers of*

12

Thomas A. Edison, Vol. 1, ed. Reese V. Jenkins et al. [Johns Hopkins University Press, 1989], p. 613)

We may not be able to understand the technical process that Edison is considering, but we can make several points about the writer-based features of this passage: it contains misspelling, erratic capitalization and punctuation, cross-outs, and technical jargon (knots is shorthand for "nautical miles"). Much of the writing is speculative and conditional—with frequent use of such words as *if*, *might*, *would*, *could*, and *try*. Edison rehearses potential experiments by putting his thinking on paper, and in so doing he makes his thoughts visible so he can reconsider them. For example, in the second paragraph he plans to "try two *insulated* disks" and then draws a line through *insulated*, perhaps because he first planned to use insulated disks but then thought of using "rubber" disks, and rubber disks eliminate the need for insulation.

Thomas Edison was a prolific practitioner of writing to learn. He used his notebooks as discovery and planning tools, not as forums for formal communication. However, when he showed some pages from his notebook to a lab associate and requested some feedback on his thinking, we can be sure he did not expect and would not appreciate the lab partner circling his errors in spelling, grammar, and punctuation and telling him that he was a poor writer. If Edison were held to writing-to-communicate standards for his notebooks, we might well conclude that he was an even worse writer than Thomas in "My Utopia." But, Edison knew the difference between writing to learn and writing to communicate. In the year 1882 alone, he applied for 107 patents or one every 3.4 days, and we can be sure these were effective examples of reader-based communication—Edison was awarded a total of 1,093 patents. Edison was successful in "explaining the matter to others" in patent applications because he first "explained the matter to himself" in his thousands of notebooks and experiments. To apply Edison's example to our teaching, students need to write to learn more than they usually do in order to reach a fuller understanding of their subject and thus be prepared to explain that understanding to others. Teachers as supportive readers might respond to students' writing to learn as Edison's lab partners might have, and they might respond to the students' writing to communicate, first as Edison's patent attorneys might have in seeking to help him improve his argument and its presentation, and second as readers in the patent office might have as they evaluate Edison's claim to an original invention.

The One-minute Essay

Once the principles are understood, there are myriad ways that teachers can use writing to learn in their classes. One example is the "one-minute essay" or the end-of-class response. At the end of class, whether it be a lecture, lab, or discussion, the teacher asks students to write for a minute (or three or four) about two things: (1) what they learned in class that day and (2) what questions or concerns they still have. A chemical engineering professor at Clemson University, Doug Hirt, collects these responses, reads them quickly before the next period, and responds individually to students. Here is Pat's one-minute essay with Doug's response **(in bold)**:

13

Today we learned about diffusion. Diffusion will take place when there is a concentration gradient. Particle diffusion is random motion along ("down") a concentration gradient. If the fluid is in motion, the velocity is due to random motion and by convection. The molar flux is the sum of the concentrations times the velocities. Looking through my notes, I can't see the difference between J_A and N. J_A is the molar flux of A and N is the total flux? So $J_A = C_A U_{Ad}$? In a two component mixture, $N_A = J_A$ only if the diffusion is equimolar in opposite directions or where the mixture is dilute in A. Flux depends on diffusion and convection.

$$N = N_A + N_B$$

J_A – with respect to coordinates moving at U_O

Flux of A

N_A – with respect to stationary coordinates

$$J_A = C_A U_{Ad}$$
$$N_A = C_A U_A$$

Although we might not understand the technical language, we can see the process at work here. Pat puts the main points of this day's lecture in his own words. In the act of reviewing the notes, Pat realizes he doesn't understand something and asks two questions. The teacher then responds specifically to Pat's questions. Pat is reviewing what he does know and what he doesn't know and then appeals to the mentoring teacher for help. Teachers like this technique for a variety of reasons: it puts them in frequent contact with students—what students are learning and what they are having difficulty with; it encourages questions that might not be voiced in front of the entire class; it promotes good listening skills because students know they will have to synthesize what they hear in their own words; it provides opportunities for students to become confident with technical vocabulary and concepts by putting it in their own language; and it promotes good student-teacher communication.

Teachers have experimented with variations on this assignment to meet their own needs. In large classes, for example, these writings are collected, but because of time limitations the teacher does not respond to each individually but rather gives an oral "collective" response at the beginning of the next class: "Here is what *I* learned from reading your one-minute essays," going on to discuss issues and questions that emerged frequently or that were particularly provocative. Other teachers do not collect the writings, at least not daily, but ask one or two students to read theirs at the beginning of the next class period—as a way of summarizing the previous lecture and seeing what questions still exist. Teachers occasionally ask students in groups of four or five to read to each other and then select one question to bring before the entire class. In this way, students hear what three or four other students think was most important about the previous lecture and hear what kinds of questions are being asked, and the teacher ensures that good questions of interest to several students get taken up by the whole class. One teacher gives closed-book and closed-notes tests but allows students to use their collection of one-minute essays during tests. Students are thus motivated to be more attentive listeners and note takers and then to write really useful one-minute essays. The more accurate the lecture summary and the more perceptive the questions (including teacher response, if any), the more valuable they will be at test time.

The Journal

Many teachers require frequent write-to-learn assignments, and the class journal is a popular tool for daily writing and reviewing. Indeed, "My Utopia" could have been the first entry in Thomas's journal, and Pat's one-minute essay could have been but one of several entries in a journal. Like Edison's notebooks, a journal is a place to write regularly, to think, organize, ask questions, work out problems. Many teachers who use journals in their classes require students to do a minimum amount of writing each week (for example, at least three 200-word entries). Entries are sometimes made during class and sometimes for homework. The subjects for writing are diverse: frequently teachers tell students some entries can be on anything they want to write about related to the course and the discipline, and at other times they specify a particular form (such as the one-minute essay) or a particular topic ("define your utopia") for an entry. This latter example I refer to as the "focused journal-write."

Here is an example of a focused journal-write from a student in Professor Diana George's art history class at Michigan Technological University. Diana asked students to read a chapter in their textbook about the Classical and the Romantic Periods in art, and then she asked them to write in their journals for homework about an unfamiliar painting—one reproduced and posted outside her office door. She encouraged the students to interpret the painting using the knowledge gained from the textbook and to feel free to include their personal reaction as well. Here is Resa's journal entry:

10/11 *Raft of the Medusa* by Gericault

By looking at this painting, you can really see the differences between the Classical Period and the Romantic Period. The first thing that really caught my attention was the emotion taking place. You can see the despair in the survivors' eyes. It kind of makes you want to reach out to these people. Where Classicism emphasizes balance, Romanticism does not. I don't think that you can really get all the emotions and action of this painting if it were in perfect balance. When you see balance, what comes into mind is order and there is no such order taking place on this raft. Another thing this painting shows that is typical of the Romantic period is that it emphasizes the spirit of the people. It does not concern itself with nationhood or only the elite public. One thing I really think is startling about this painting are the men who are kind of hanging off the raft. This probably enhances the emotions taking place but I really don't think the man in the lower right corner fits in very well. It seems overly dramatized, the way his leg is hugging that log seems a little too played up.

What Resa has done is attempt to make sense of her reading experience and her viewing experience. She is attempting to learn concepts unfamiliar to her (such as Romantic) and how a knowledge of such concepts provides one way of making distinctions and acquiring knowledge, insight, and a critical perspective about art. She is not just memorizing definitions to regurgitate back to the teacher on a test. She is trying on the technical vocabulary of the art historian but also registering her personal judgment. Based on her reading of Resa's and the other students' journal entries during this time, Diana designed additional "focused journal-writes" to help students critique the characteristics of Classical and Romantic found in the textbook. How accurate and useful are these conceptions for thinking about art? What are their limitations as well as their strengths? Thus, Diana uses writing to learn to help students develop their interpretive and critical thinking abilities.

Here is some advice on using journals in classes. Require students to write in a small looseleaf notebook. It should be small, about 5" x 8", so student writers will be encouraged to carry it around with them and jot down ideas whenever they occur, much as Thomas Edison did. Unless a teacher has another educational purpose, such as teaching the protocol of the scientific notebook that, for legal reasons, must be sewn, a looseleaf notebook often works best. With a looseleaf notebook, a teacher like Diana can collect one page from each student to see what each makes of Gericault, or she can collect as many entries as she has time to read. She can ask students to divide their journal into two sections, academic and personal, in which the first includes their understanding of the readings, slides, and lectures and the second includes reactions and connections to their personal lives.

Teachers often wonder where they will find the time to read and respond to all this writing, but there are legitimate ways to cut the time required. Students who write thirty pages in their journal by midterm can be asked to select the six or seven pages to which they would like a response and submit only those, or students can be asked occasionally to submit their entire journals but to put an asterisk at the top of the three or four pages where they want the reader to slow down, read more carefully, and provide a response. Such a technique encourages students to reread their journals and make an assessment about which sections are most important to them. I used to say that it is more important that students do this kind of writing to learn than that teachers read it. I now realize just how important it is for most students to receive interactive response from the teacher (or others), but I also realize that students can help focus that response in meaningful and time-saving ways.

Journals are flexible tools, and teachers enjoy experimenting with them to help students meet course goals. For example, some teachers concerned about students' critical reading abilities require double-sided journals. In such journals, students draw a line down the middle of each page, and as they read each section of an assigned text, they briefly summarize or identify the main points on the left side of their journal page and then briefly note questions, personal connections, and interpretations on the right side.

But probably my best advice on journals is to make regular, frequent use of them in class. Teachers new to journals sometimes assign them on the first day of class, require maybe three entries a week, and then don't mention them again until midterm. When they read them, they realize that the journals are the product of a marathon writing session the night before, complete with properly identified different dates. Journals need to be integrated into the fabric of a course. Individual pages (like Resa's) can be collected and responded to before midterm, journal-writes (like Thomas's) can be used as a basis for a brainstorming session, one-minute essays (like Pat's) can be the basis for an ongoing student-teacher dialogue about chemical engineering, classes can begin with each person (students and teacher) doing some journal writing on the subject of that day's class, and students can read last night's journal entry to each other (however, always let them know in advance the possible audiences for journal entries). Students learn that journals are valuable, not just "busywork," because they are used daily as students and teacher build the knowledge of the course.

Writing Poetry

Researchers reading the voluminous notebooks of Thomas Edison were surprised to find that he occasionally used them to write poetry or to do humorous drawings—that he used his notebooks for work and for play. I've often thought that if language and thinking are connected in some way, then creative language use might be connected to creative thinking and problem solving, to alternative and innovative ways of seeing and doing. Creative writing across the curriculum posits that students can benefit from writing creatively in any course because such language can generate new and fresh perspectives, develop creative language abilities, and provide a better understanding of the various functions of written language. Creative writing assignments can function in most classes the way other writing-to-learn strategies do—as opportunities to make discoveries about the material under study and to increase the quality and the quantity of student-teacher interaction. When a biology or accounting professor introduces creative writing into a class, the purpose is not to make students novelists or poets, but to provide creative connections and learning opportunities about the material under study. Creative writing may mean stories, plays, parables, songs, analogies, and so on; here I discuss the possibility of introducing an occasional poetry assignment into a course.

The following poem is by Melissa, who was enrolled in accounting Professor Lew Bryan's auditing class at Clemson University. In preparation for writing a poem, students discussed possible subjects, one of which was "what it might be like to be an auditor."

An Auditor's Love

The elevator opened and there she stood.
She was dressed to impress as no one else could.

Her eyes sparkled like a flash of light.
You knew in your heart it was love at first sight.

The elevator ride was just like a dream.
She was the only one for you, so it seemed.

You went to your office and to your surprise,
In walked the lady with sparkling eyes.

You promised her dinner and a kiss good night,
But deep in her heart she knows it's not right.

You promised to take her on a cruise around the world,
But she is your auditor, she can't be your girl.

She has signed a code of ethics, and these rules are not flexible; they won't even
    bend;
So before the romance starts, it must come to an end.

There is no such thing as an auditor's love.

Melissa's poem is interesting to read from a variety of perspectives, and her professor and classmates *enjoyed* it. In the poem, she considers what it would be like to be a female auditor assigned temporarily to audit a corporate client, the issue of gender politics in such a workplace, the line between an intimate relationship and being emotionally used or financially bribed, and the code of ethics that distinguishes between self-interest and professionalism that she has been learning about in class. And she does so with imagination, cleverness, and a wry sense of humor—and in 150 words. Such brief poems often allow students and teachers to imagine and discuss important topics and perspectives that other classroom talk and writing would not, especially in technical courses like auditing.

Another example, a poem by Ryan, comes from Professor Darrell Yardley's biology course, which studied DNA and the theory of evolution. Darrell told his class that "poetry was no big deal" and not to spend more than thirty minutes writing a poem.

Nature's Legos

The spiral of life—DNA
What are its mysteries; Who can say?

What causes cancer, curse to the young and to the old?
And what of deformation and mutation; the story may never be told.

DNA is both the key to the future and the key to the past.
The information coded in such a tiny thing is so increadably vast!

Was it created by God or by natural selection?
Regardless, shouldn't life be more than just a subject for reflexion?

Adenine to thymine and cytosine to guanine linked up and down the spiral stair.
Another young child is born and another old child is dead,
Does nature really care?

Ryan uses the opportunity created by the assignment to reflect on the new knowledge he is learning about DNA and the questions it raises for him (as it has for others). Again, this is a writing-to-learn assignment, done in 112 words, easy for the teacher and for classmates to read. On a test, Ryan may need to demonstrate his knowledge of adenine and thymine; in a poem, he has the opportunity to link them to questions about the meaning of life. Even though serious, Ryan plays with language and uses the oxymoron "old child" as a metaphor for all humanity in the expanse of time posited by the theory of evolution. Yes, he has misspelled *incredibly* and *reflection*, but the purpose of the assignment was to experiment with words and ideas within a friendly classroom context, not to write a piece of formal communication. Ryan has time constraints also—the purpose of the assignment was to generate a poem in thirty minutes or less for classmates to read, not to polish a highly crafted poem for publication.

Mike Gorman, a former professor of psychology at Michigan Tech and now at the University of Virginia, often assigned poems in his introductory psychology classes, which frequently enrolled 75 to 100 students. In the assignment for which Suzette wrote the following poem, he asked students to empathize with persons suffering from mental illness or with the health professionals that care for them.

> She came in my office
> In yellow from top to bottom
>
> "I dream of macaroni & cheese"
> she said
> This was her favorite food
> But later
> I concluded that
> What she was really doing
> was being *that* food
>
> Reality
> was school
> Bio tests and Lab
> Steve the TA
> gives another quiz
> "Take me home, Kraft"
>
> What an escape!
> Thin, white, and hollow
> She puts on her yellow
> sweatshirt
> Then on goes the cheese
> And all is well.

In my opinion, Suzette has written a very moving poem about a college student suffering from some sort of depression and the metaphoric interpretation the counselor gives to her condition. From the counselor's point of view, the student is trying to escape from reality, from the pressures of college studies, by entering her own yellow dream world of macaroni and cheese. The contrast between the starchy, fattening, yellow macaroni and cheese and the student, described as "Thin, white, and hollow," conjures up an image of anorexia as well as depression. The metaphor is made all the more chilling by the recognition that "Thin, white and hollow" refers not only to the mentally ill student in her yellow sweatshirt but also to a noodle of macaroni before the cheese goes on. You may not agree with me that this is a moving poem, but it does not matter in this educational context. Readers are not called upon to make judgments about such poetry nor are teachers required to assign grades to it; we are asked only to read it and see if it moves us, to see if this brief exercise makes any difference for teacher, writer, or classmates. In this course, Suzette is studying psychology, not learning to write poetry. Mike wanted students not only to have a scientific understanding of how the mind works and sometimes malfunctions (which he could verify by tests and formal reports) but also to have empathy for the human beings behind the statistics and the technical jargon. In seventy-six well-chosen words, Suzette helps us experience our humanity.

Many students, of course, have a wonderful sense of humor. For many teachers, because of large classes or other reasons, this aspect of students' perspectives on knowledge is never revealed. I conclude this section with a forty-three word poem by Sonja, a student in Mike Gorman's educational psychology course. Students were studying various theoretical and social aspects of IQ testing and he asked that they write brief poems.

Some men are super macho
And always do their besty
But the proof of real manhood
Is in their IQ testes.

IQ "60" men don't turn me on
"100" men be damned
To really turn this girl on
It takes a mensa man.

I am not suggesting that poetry and other creative assignments be used frequently in all courses. If they were, they would quickly become stale and routine for teachers and students. I do, however, lament that such creative language experiences are practically nonexistent in this country after about grade six, unless a student enrolls specifically in a creative writing course. I'm convinced that occasional, purposeful creative writing assignments make a valuable contribution to students' understanding of the subject matter under study, usually from a perspective not included in tests or formal reports, and that they make a contribution to students' language development. Students employ humor, irony, and language play, and they use metaphor and analogy for expression and thought. They exercise their imaginations, they reach out to readers, and they express values and concerns that relate the course material to their lives. Even Sonja, the writer of the humorous IQ poem, when asked to comment on the experience of writing this poem, refers to her values and personal perspective: "I had fun writing this. Though it is sarcastic, that's how I feel IQ tests tend to be used—in a ridiculous manner. Comparison is healthy to a certain point but I feel they've overextended their usefulness and sometimes cause a great deal of harm."

Writing Notes

One writing-to-learn technique grew directly out of the WAC workshops and the supportive WAC program we have at Clemson. Dan McAuliff, who teaches electrical engineering, and I began a conversation at one of our WAC workshops and continued it at lunch a week later. Dan was considering integrating writing into his basic electrical engineering course, a junior-level course on electric circuit theory required of non-EE majors in the College of Engineering. In this course, which usually enrolls 80 to 100 students each semester, Dan was not interested in adding a lengthy technical report to the students' workload or his. Indeed, as we talked, Dan developed two goals for writing assignments. First, he wanted students to write as a way of developing a basic understanding of electric circuits. Second, he hoped the writing would help students overcome the fear and anxiety that many exhibited because of the unfamiliar course material. As we talked, we decided to develop write-to-learn assignments that would confront the isolation, the anxiety, the feeling of being out of their element (sorry, I just couldn't resist that pun), that many students felt and that often interfered with their ability to grasp concepts and to work problems. Dan decided to have students write "notes" back and forth to each other. He described "notes" as being not as informal as journal entries—written to the self, but not as formal as memos—which are usually typed and filed for future reference. Notes could be handwritten and passed easily to a colleague for quick response. Dan and I then developed a collaborative version of the one-minute essay.

Four times during the semester, students would write a note summarizing what they understood about the concept being studied at that time and where they had difficulties and questions. Then, instead of the teacher responding individually, the students exchanged notes and responded to each other at the very next class. Dan sequenced the assignments like this: Tuesday, first note due; Thursday, response to fellow student's note due; Tuesday, exam on the material. Dan required each note to be at least 200 words long and submitted in two copies: one for the fellow student and one for him. Here is an example of a note (edited for length only) written just before a test on DC circuit analysis.

1/30 Bill,

The most difficult thing I find about DC circuit analysis is keeping up with the sign conventions. I find the sign convention can be confusing because it treats a voltage drop as a positive quantity in the direction of current flow. After all, when one considers a drop one usually thinks of a negative quantity. The voltage source provides a voltage rise, yet, using the established sign convention a voltage source must be considered as a negative drop and hence a negative quantity.   Terry

Terry writes about some of the difficulties and the confusion he is experiencing in trying to think about and work with circuitry. In so doing, Terry understands better his own thought processes and the nature of his difficulties—a good experience in its own right because it lessens the feeling of being overwhelmed in this new field of study. On Tuesday, Terry gives Bill the note, and on Thursday Bill responds.

21

2/1 Terry,

I completely empathize with your position. It's a shame that such a fundamental concept stumps us all, but recently I stumbled across our explanation.

As with most things in nature, electricity flows from a high concentration to a lower concentration. This flow from high to low can be considered a "drop." As water flows over a water-fall the energy of the water as it hits the ground is dependent upon the height of the fall. Consider the voltage to be represented by the height of the fall. The greater the voltage the higher the fall and the greater the drop which is a positive value.

Concerning the aspect of the sign on convention for voltage in DC circuit analysis, recall Kirchhof voltage law. Restated, for a one-loop circuit, the algebraic sum of the component voltages is equal to the source. Thus for the following circuit:

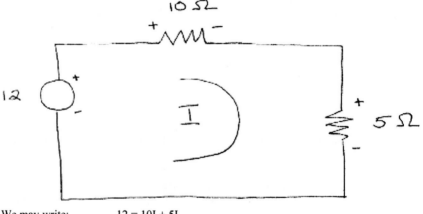

We may write: $12 = 10I + 5I$

or as we usually write $0 = 10I + 5I - 12$

So we can see that the sign convention is dependent upon the mathematical manipulator not electrical concepts.

Bill begins his response with a rhetorical recognition of his audience, Terry, and a reference to their common experience in this difficult and unfamiliar course. He then goes on to use a standard problem-solving technique: develop an analogy in which the unfamiliar is compared to the familiar. Bill's wonderful analogy of the "water-fall" speaks directly to the conceptual confusion that Terry was experiencing about the apparently illogical flow of electricity. His second analogy is more technical but nonetheless appropriate. He takes the unfamiliar "electrical concepts" and shows how they follow familiar mathematical logic. In writing his response, Bill may well have reviewed his notes and his textbook, but he was applying what he learned in a very specific context—to help a fellow engineer-in-training. I also believe that Bill himself has learned something in writing this response. By articulating his analogies, and making his thinking visible, both Bill and Terry are more likely to remember what they have learned and more likely to apply it in the kinds of unexpected ways that often confront engineers working on the job.

Dan collected a photocopy of these writings at the same time the student passed them to one another. Students who followed the assignment, that is, turned in all eight notes promptly, in two copies, at least 200 words each, with reasonable effort to fulfill the assignment, received full credit. Each teacher who uses such techniques should decide how much credit and how to grade or count such writings within the context of his or her own course goals. Dan felt no need to circle or deduct points because Bill had misspelled *waterfall* or *Kirchhoff*, but he did deduct points from students who did not fulfill the assignment, who wrote things like "I don't understand anything about DC circuit analysis" and thereby gave their partners no manageable way to respond.

Dan and I are convinced that these notes were valuable writing-to-learn exercises for his students, and we also believe that the students learned something as well about writing-to-communicate: they wrote to help a real person with a real problem. Bill was one of many students to begin a note by establishing a tone to put the reader at ease—stating that it is okay to have difficulty understanding electrical circuits, that working together we can help one another to understand them better, that we can bring our personal language into a technical course to help us learn the unfamiliar language of electrical engineering, that we can use our personal knowledge of waterfalls as a way to think about technical concepts.

These note assignments were valuable to Dan as well. He would collect them and skim through them quickly, reading to assess how these notes helped students learn electrical concepts; he also read them to see what difficulties students were having in understanding the material and to see how they were helping one another with those difficulties. Dan would make an occasional remark on a student's note, but with teaching as many as 100 students, he did not attempt to provide an individual response (that was the responsibility of a classmate). Rather, he provided the class with a "collective response." After reading a set of notes, he would begin the next class period by informing the students about what he had learned as he read their writing: suggesting how to improve their notes ("be as specific as you can about your difficulties"); summarizing the most frequently mentioned difficulties—and his willingness to spend more time on them; and thoughts that were useful to him personally— such as Bill's waterfall analogy. He sometimes read sections from particularly interesting notes to the entire class, either because they addressed challenging issues or because they might make good models for other students to emulate in future writing. Thus, the students received a variety of meaningful responses to their notes: a lengthy, written, individual response on specific issues from a classmate and a considered, oral, collective response from Dan, the teacher as mentor. And the students experienced the fact that their writing made a difference—that a classmate took it seriously as an intellectual challenge, that their teacher sometimes changed the course structure in response to it (such as making time to review a particular problem), that the entire process helped them better understand electrical engineering.

Both Dan and I on different occasions have presented the concept of the "note exchange" to our colleagues at Clemson during subsequent WAC workshops. Inevitably, a participant asks: "What if a student answers a fellow student's note with a totally inaccurate answer?" Shouldn't the teacher intervene, take time to set the writer straight, warn the unsuspecting reader about the bad advice? And if so, doesn't this take a lot of time in a class with a hundred students? Certainly, each teacher needs to decide how to handle such issues within the context of her or his class. But Dan and I are both comfortable with the following practice: occasionally intervene and help students, but do not set yourself up as a constant checkpoint. A major point of writing to learn is for students to be responsible for their own learning. Each time a student receives a return note, that student should judge the accuracy and value of the information. We don't want to encourage students to get answers from fellow students and then repeat by rote, without understanding, those solutions on tests. When a student receives a response, he or she should see for himself or herself if it has value—by working some problems or considering possible applications. The student needs to decide, as he or she will on the job, whether the advice was totally worthless, somewhat helpful, or accurate. So Dan made no attempt to check the accuracy of every note each student had written. But because he recognized differences in students' interest and ability, he required different partners for each note exchange, thus allowing students to experience various approaches to problem solving.

In using the note exchange with hundreds of students over five semesters, Dan found that approximately 90 percent of the students found them to be valuable and recommended that they continue to be a part of the course. About 5 percent refused to take them seriously or found them of little use. Dan collected this information by requiring that the final note of each semester be addressed to him and that it discuss (again, in a minimum of 200 words) the student's experience with the note assignments. These final notes have been enormously useful to Dan and me as we consider further possibilities for writing-to-learn and group problem-solving strategies. Here is Susan's:

4/1 Mr. McAuliff,

These homework assignments have contributed greatly to my understanding of electrical engineering concepts. I must admit, at first I was very skeptical and viewed them as more "busy work." I have been pleased and quite surprised about the outcome.

Before I took this class, I did not know anything about electrical engineering. These assignments proved that I was not alone in my fears. This put me more at ease and less reluctant to ask questions. In addition, I developed a much better attitude toward this class which in turn helped my grades.

From reading several of my classmates assignments, I finally realized the physical meaning of electric circuits and I was able to make analogies with mechanical systems and their equations of motion.

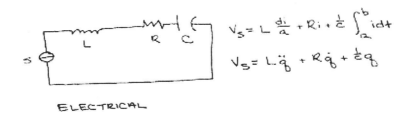

$$V_s = L\frac{di}{dt} + Ri + \frac{1}{C}\int_a^b i\,dt$$

$$V_s = L\ddot{q} + R\dot{q} + \frac{1}{C}q$$

ELECTRICAL

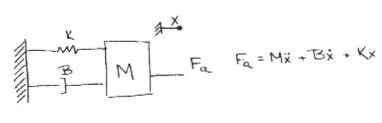

$$F_a = M\ddot{x} + B\dot{x} + Kx$$

MECHANICAL

This example shows that the voltage acts like an applied force, inductance like a mass, resistance like a damper, capacitance like a spring, and charge like displacement. This analogy could prove to be very beneficial in the future to mechanical engineers, as well as civil engineers, who are trying to understand electrical circuits.

Susan expresses ideas shared by many of her classmates. In the first two paragraphs, she gives her general reaction. She admits she was skeptical of writing tasks, since her experience suggests that school-based assignments are "busywork," which I take to mean not useful. She is therefore "surprised" to find that the notes have contributed "greatly" to her understanding of electrical engineering concepts. The notes have decreased her alienation and fears and improved her attitude (and grades) in the class. For Susan, a mechanical engineering major, Dan's two goals for the note assignments have been met: to help students learn electric circuits and to help students overcome their anxiety about having to learn electrical engineering. Her general testimony is very flattering, but it also might be mostly what I call "teachereez." Teachereez is when students tell teachers what they think teachers want to hear. However, in the third and fourth paragraphs, Susan moves from a general to a personal and particular assessment—one not easily faked to please the teacher.

Susan relates how she was able to create an analogy that made electric circuits accessible to her. She credits her breakthrough not to the textbook or to the teacher's lectures, but rather to "reading several of my classmates assignments," which enabled her to make both verbal and visual analogies of electric circuits to mechanical systems. As a mechanical engineer, she knows equations of motion, and she uses the conceptual parallels to electric circuits to make the unfamiliar familiar. And she credits her initiative to become such an active, creative, responsible thinker and problem solver to the written exchanges between students and the supportive classroom environment that encouraged them. In her last sentence, she gives Dan a teaching suggestion—that her analogy might be "very beneficial in the future" as he teaches mechanical and civil engineers about electric circuits, and indeed it has been. However, Dan does not spoon-feed future students with analogies from previous classes; he would much rather they learn to think and express their own.

Another student, Holly, wrote that "the note responses required more than pulling your book off the shelf and thumbing through it for the answer. They required what most every student hates—thinking! So while understanding the material, I was still having to take the time to think. Terrible, huh?" What Holly is saying, I take it, is that these assignments required active learning and not passive regurgitation, that, in Susan's words, they were not the usual "busy work" of much college writing. Holly makes a distinction that we read many times over in the students' notes to Dan, a distinction between having to understand the material and to think about it. Most college assignments require students to "understand" the material (memorize it) and to demonstrate that fleeting knowledge by displaying it on a quiz or lab report. But these notes require thinking, creativity, application, contextualization, all things college students "hate" to do! College students, like the rest of us, would rather take shortcuts to a grade. When students such as Susan and Holly provide such assessments at the end of a term, they give teachers one of the best reality checks on our assignments' effectiveness.

Just as Dan created a classroom environment conducive to good work, our Clemson WAC program also creates a conducive campus environment. Since Dan began experimenting with notes in electrical engineering, numerous other faculty in various disciplines have done so as well. Indeed, Melanie Cooper, who teaches introductory chemistry in sections of 200, and Robert Jamison, who teaches advanced courses in mathematics in sections of 25, have both adapted this technique to their courses and then given presentations about the process at subsequent WAC workshops and professional meetings. Because every classroom presents a different context, we must experiment with how WAC techniques might work in our situation. Yet such experimentation thrives in an environment in which it evolves in collaboration with colleagues across campus who participate in a WAC program. Dan and I continue to meet for lunch to discuss our teaching experiments, and we also meet regularly at follow-up WAC workshops. What I learned from Dan, Melanie, Robert, and others led me to adapt the notes experiment to my upper-level Victorian literature course.

Writing Letters

I've experimented with letters in the classes I teach. The concept is the same as in the notes assignments, a letter exchange between pairs of students. While I wanted students to use the personal voice associated with letters, I also wanted to encourage the movement to a more academic and critical use of language. Thus, from one perspective, I created a space between informal writing-to-learn assignments and formal writing-to-communicate assignments. Here is the context for the letter exchange in my Victorian literature class. It was the last of six writing assignments students were required to do. Two of the other assignments were formal critical essays on the literature, and three were informal creative assignments, such as writing a poem in the dramatic

26

monologue form of Robert Browning. Students kept their writing in a portfolio, which was read and assessed by them and by me about midterm and at the course conclusion.

For this final assignment, students had one week to read the novel *Heart of Darkness* by Joseph Conrad and to read one scholarly essay by Chinua Achebe, who argues that the novel is racist. Part 1 of this assignment, the first letter, was written to a partner about the problems encountered in interpreting the novel, and it was written before the novel was discussed in class. It could be handwritten and was to be about 200 words long. Part 2, the response letter, which suggested possible answers and perhaps raised other issues to be discussed, was written following a week's class discussion and needed to be typed and be about 500 words long. Students knew as well that there would be a final exam question on *Heart of Darkness.*

Here is the exchange between Emily and Alyson:

Alyson,

On page 149, Marlow makes a general statement about women after having a conversation with his aunt, saying, "It's queer how out of touch with truth women are. They live in a world of their own, and there has never been anything like it, and never can be. It is too beautiful altogether, and if they were to set it up, it would go to pieces before the first sunset." After reading the novel, I could see how Marlow would think that Kurtz's Intended fit into this stereotype. She did really seem to be totally out of touch with reality, and she didn't seem to have a clue about the man she loved. The question I want to ask is whether the African woman described near the end of the novel on page 226 fits into this stereotype? Actually, I would like to know where and how she fits into the novel at all, beyond the insinuations of being Kurtz's mistress. I think this woman must be symbolic of something, although I am not exactly sure of what. Is she a living, breathing human embodiment of the "heart of darkness," the wilderness of the African Congo, as seems to be indicated on page 226?

-Emily

Emily's letter to Alyson refers to specific passages in the novel by page number, attempts to synthesize these passages around the issue of how women are portrayed in the novel, and then asks specific questions related to the "African woman." Emily contextualizes her question in terms of her own experience with the novel. She describes for Alyson what she understands as well as where she still has questions. She has given Alyson a lot to think about. A week later, Alyson responds.

Emily,

In class, we discussed the possibility that *Heart of Darkness* is a masculine novel. This idea seems supported by the narrator's reliance on patriarchal assumptions and Marlow's unsympathetic view of women and perhaps, by the subject matter which focuses on plotting, murder, intrigue and male adventure. Based on these assumptions, the savage woman's role can be explained as a symbolic representation of the things to which this man feels alternately attracted and repulsed—woman and Africa.

Before the trip, Marlow has, as you mentioned, stated his demeaning and subordinating attitude towards women (that they're out of touch with truth). But that description fits his Aunt and the Intended specifically, while this savage woman seems a striking deviation from this stereotype. When considering the savage woman in the context of Marlow's stereotype, I came up with several possibilities.

Some possibilities for the purpose of this woman were suggested briefly by Achebe. He believes that she serves as a direct contrast or opposite to the Intended. If so, I wonder why Conrad would deliberately draw this contrast with his own view of woman who is embodied in the Intended? When you consider the dichotomies presented (Thames/ Congo, Africa/England, civilized/savage, good/evil), this contrast of the powerful, wild savage with the civilized, naive Intended is a fitting echo of the division being made by Marlow. But does Marlow's image of women represent what he wants them to be? I think it does because he willfully hides the truth from the Intended by lying about Kurtz's last words.

Yet I think it's important that, to Marlow, truth is available to men only. It is a masculine concern. So if the woman represents Africa, which he suggests is the case by such comments as ". . .the whole sorrowful land. . . .seemed to look at her, pensive, as though it had been looking at the image of its own tenebrous and passionate soul" (76), then she has a strong connection with truth. As I see it, the primitive and savage is the vehicle for truth in *Heart of Darkness*; therefore, this woman conveys, or threatens to convey, truth. . . .

However, another purpose this woman serves is to help explain Kurtz. The implication that she was his mistress makes Marlow and the reader consider her as a real woman, one who is capable of having a relationship with a white man. It's interesting to consider whether Conrad created her to represent how savage Kurtz had become or to show us that our kinship with Africa is real. I think an important question is whether she represents a positive alternative to the deluded, meek Intended or whether she represents the darkness which lured Kurtz into madness. That question asks, I think, a major decision to be made about the novel.

-Alyson

Alyson's thoughtful response speaks directly to the issues raised by Emily, and she provides several informed observations about the general role of women in the novel and about the role of the African woman in particular. Although she writes a letter to Emily and addresses Emily's personal and very specific concerns about the novel, Alyson's language is thoughtfully academic. She integrates Achebe's interpretation into the flow of her letter, questions and then challenges it, and uses it to further her own discussion on *Heart of Darkness.*

As I read the thirty-five pairs of letters exchanged by the students, the first thing that struck me was the quality of the writing about literature they exhibited: the questions and issues raised for critical thinking, the insight and agility with the process of literary interpretation, the impressive array of intellectual skills that was brought to bear in assisting one another to understand the novel: analysis, synthesis, inference and speculation, integration of primary and secondary sources.

Why was I surprised by such engagement and sophistication by my students? Because these letters contrasted markedly with the two formal critical essays they had written previously in the course—which were not coherent or insightful. I began to question what might have caused this difference in quality:

the shift in audience from teacher as primary to fellow student as primary (with teacher as secondary)? the shift in context, from a topic designed by the teacher to a question raised by a fellow student? the shift from the specialized form and language of literary criticism—an unfamiliar language that many students pretend they have mastered—to the form and language of letters, at once personal and familiar?

Some other questions I muse about when I study this writing: Why did the students complain about the restrictions on their creativity and their interpretive ability when I assigned the broad topic of love in Oscar Wilde's *The Importance of Being Earnest* for their critical essay and not complain at all about writing a letter to a fellow student on a much narrower topic, such as the "role of African woman" in *Heart of Darkness*, who appears for only a couple of pages? And why, at the end of class, on the student evaluation form did numerous students comment that the letters were the most difficult writing assignment of the term and the most time-consuming, and yet the one they found most valuable and learned the most from?

I don't have answers to these questions, but I do have some initial speculations. First, I think the social nature of the assignment was important. The students had interpreted my "critical essay" assignment as the familiar school assignment, what Susan called "busy work"—show the teacher that you read *The Importance of Being Earnest* and can think of some things to say about it. You are not really helping the teacher understand the play any better because the teacher has read and taught the play several times, read many professional books and essays about it, and you have spent a week reading this play while taking four or five other classes at the same time. The advantage of the letters is that they are written for a specific individual, a peer, who is asking real questions, asking for help, and for whom you can play the role of colleague or teacher as mentor. The letters demonstrate students communicating to a real audience rather than practicing at communicating to the pretend audience of professional scholars who read and write essays about literature. In addition, the letters are contextualized within the classroom community. As you can see from Alyson's response letter—and this was true of most letters—the classroom lectures, discussions, and readings are integrated into the letter writing. Students synthesize and make sense of what they heard and read in class. The formal critical essays were written in a vacuum, as if to mention that you got some of your ideas from classmates and class discussion was a form of cheating. The letter assignment, I believe, was vital to the knowledge students were gaining, while the critical essay was perceived as an "add-on assignment"—out-of-class project—and became, in practice, an isolated and isolating task.

Second, I think the problem-posing nature of the assignment was important. The students learned in writing part 1 of the assignment just as they did in writing the longer and more formal part 2. Fundamental to every discipline is figuring out how to ask important and germane questions that continue the advancement of knowledge within that field. You must be knowledgeable to ask good questions (and I discovered that my students were knowledgeable), and good questions beget good responses. And the person writing back to you knows that superficial generalities or a string of quotes from secondary sources will not do—will not answer your questions and address your confusion, will not help you understand a little more about *Heart of Darkness*. It places responsibility on the writer of part 2, an obligation to teach, an obligation to be sincere and honest. Alyson responds sincerely to Emily by asking several important questions herself, and these questions and the insightful conclusion to her essay become an invitation to continue the conversation, not an attempt to provide definitive answers and thus end it.

In reading my students' writing—both the critical essays and the letter exchange—I not only learn about the students, about Oscar Wilde and Joseph Conrad, but also I learn about myself as a teacher, who and what I value in teaching. I now realize I prefer my mirrored reflection, my own self-image, as it is represented in the student letters—rather than the image of me I see represented in their critical essays. This does not mean that formal essays always make poor assignments, but rather that I need to improve the way I design and use such essays in my classes. I am continually challenged to be an effective teacher by what I learn about teaching with writing from colleagues across the disciplines, from students, and from observing my own teaching.

Designing Writing-to-learn Assignments

This summary sheet that I distribute at faculty workshops may be useful to you.

■ Designing writing-to-learn assignments

Goals:

- Integrate into important course work, not "add on" or "busy work"
- Promote active learning and interactive learning
- Encourage critical reflection and transference of skills and knowledge
- Improve classroom community and learning environment
- Integrate with reading, talking, listening, visualizations

Guidelines:

- Consider your goals for the course: connect writing to goals
- Consider purpose, audience and context of assignment
- Consider time (how much? teacher? students?) and place: in-class, out-of-class, botanical garden, laboratory
- Consider the form of assignment: quick write, journal entry, abstract, letter, email exchange, poem, questions, weblog, quick sketch, summary, critique, discussion board, microtheme, analysis, critical reflection

Questions:

- How will assignment promote mastery of knowledge or its applications, metacognitive reflection ("thinking about thinking"), develop students' critical thinking abilities, creativity, and/or communication skills?
- How will you use it in course: discussion, paired readers, group work, test preparation, read to class, connect to other material, show examples on overhead or computer screen, connect to lecture, lead to formal writing, scaffold learning tasks?
- What guidelines will you give students for assignments?
- How long should the writing be? How long should students work on it?
- How will you or others read and respond to these writings?
- How will you be "teacher as mentor" rather than "teacher as examiner"?
- How will you "count" or grade these writings, if at all?
- What results do you expect? What will make a successful assignment?
- How does this assignment(s) relate to other assignments and goals of the course?

In conclusion, I sometimes think the best piece of advice that I've given over the years about assignment design is "Assign only that writing you want to read." If you don't want to take home and read fifty summaries of chapter 10 of the physics textbook or seventy-five essays on the War of the Roses, then don't assign it in the first place. If you have little interest in reading student writing, chances are that students will have little interest in writing it. Under such conditions, we teachers create a situation in which writers who don't want to write, write for readers who don't want to read, and we do this in the name of improving communication. This is, indeed, busywork for both students and teachers. Rather, writing across the curriculum suggests that we begin by creating assignments and a classroom environment where students and teachers are eager to read one another's work.

■ Chapter 3: Communication Across the Curriculum

When I moved from Michigan Technological University and its WAC program in 1987, I began planning a similar program for my new school, Clemson University. As I considered the particular needs of Clemson, a land-grant university of around 17,000 students, I also reflected on what I had learned during the previous decade about WAC at Michigan Tech and on numerous visits to other campuses. In collaboration with my new colleagues at Clemson, we instituted a Communication-Across-the-Curriculum (CAC) program. With the change in name from WAC to CAC, we continued to envision writing as central to the academic experience, but we also wanted to recognize the importance of oral communication, visual communication, digital communication, critical thinking, collaboration, problem-based learning, and other active learning strategies. Indeed, WAC has always included such an integrated conception of learning and communication, as the many examples throughout this booklet demonstrate, such as the engineering students, Bill and Terry, exchanging notes that included a graphic to enable their thinking and communication (22-25). By naming our program Communication Across the Curriculum, we made explicit our goal of effectively integrating communication—written, oral, visual, electronic—throughout the curriculum.

Conversational Learning

Please take a moment and refer to my chart (9) in which I categorize two useful functions of written language in educational contexts: writing to learn and writing to communicate. WAC suggests teachers use writing for these two not mutually exclusive purposes: "writing to learn," in which emphasis is placed on using written language to learn new and unfamiliar content or to develop analytical or creative habits of mind, and "writing to communicate" to demonstrate how much has been learned or to get things done. In other words, in writing to learn, mistakes, false starts, hallelujahs, connections, and misconceptions all are viewed as part of the process by which learners learn. Most WAC proponents believe that these two functions should be integral to all writing-intensive courses, and they often label them informal and formal writing or expressive and transactional writing. They view these two functions not as totally distinct but as existing on a continuum in which some of the writing we do in classrooms falls in the middle. Indeed, when I provided the examples of Alyson and Emily's letters about *Heart of Darkness*, I wrote that I had created a space on my chart "between informal writing-to-learn assignments and formal writing-to-communicate assignments" (27). With the advent of online communication, this "middle ground" has gained a more prominent focus, because much of online writing exhibits characteristics of conversation: interactive, context dependent, reality based, rapid, colloquial, personal, audience specific, and mutually enabling in order to move the conversation forward. Such interchanges, written and oral, are often characterized as "conversational learning."

Electronic Communication Across the Curriculum

With the growing accessibility of college students and faculty to e-mail, online course management systems, and the World Wide Web, the WAC movement continues to grow and change to make full use of these emerging technologies in support of its educational goals. This development, which Donna Reiss, Dickie Selfe, and I have called Electronic Communication Across the Curriculum (ECAC), has encouraged many more faculty to participate in efforts to improve student learning and communication abilities because of their interest in integrating interactive computer technology and distance learning strategies into their courses (*Electronic Communication Across the Curriculum*, eds. Donna Reiss, Dickie Selfe, and Art Young. Urbana, IL: National Council of Teachers of English, 1998). Eventually the impact of this rapidly developing and changing communication technology will lead to a rethinking of educational goals and the theories and teaching practices that support them. Meanwhile, WAC, CAC, and ECAC are consistent in supporting the improvement of student learning and communication abilities through interactive, language-based strategies that promote active inquiry, sincere communication, collaboration, and problem solving. Thus, many of the teaching activities described in the earlier sections of this booklet can be adapted to electronic media: one-minute essays can be sent to listservs; journals can become electronic journals or weblogs; freewrites become digital "braindumps"; notes and letters can be e-mail exchanges; drafts of formal writing can be critiqued by writers in the same class or in other classes at the same college or at other colleges; and portfolios can become digital. This compatibility does not mean that everyone should convert all paper and oral assignments to electronic assignments, for there are many advantages to paper and oral assignments, but that experimenting with ECAC assignments need not require an essential rethinking of WAC theory and pedagogy by those committed to it. Indeed, many teachers unfamiliar with WAC are discovering its possibilities out of their desire to incorporate communications technology into their instruction.

The Middle Ground

In order to help myself visualize this middle ground of conversational language and learning, I developed the following chart as parallel to the earlier one on page 9. It has helped me in designing assignments consistent with my course goals and in responding to my students' writing, for it makes more explicit the rhetorical space between personal and pubic writing. (An earlier version of this chart and much of this ECAC discussion are in a book chapter I co-authored with Donna Reiss, "WAC Wired: Electronic Communication Across the Curriculum," in *WAC for the New Millennium*, eds. Susan McLeod, Eric Miraglia, Margot Soven, and Christopher Thaiss, NCTE, 2001: 63).

Classroom Discourse and Communication Across the Curriculum

	Personal Discourse	Classroom Discourse	Public Discourse
Function	**Expressive Writing** ▪ Self-discovery ▪ Inner speech	**Interactive Writing** ▪ Conversational ▪ Dialectical	**Transactional Writing** ▪ Informative ▪ Persuasive
Purpose	Explains to Oneself	Explains to Classroom Colleagues	Explains to Distant Others
Audience	**Self and Trusted Others** ▪ Privileges Language of Learner ▪ Accountability to Self	**Classroom Community: Familiar and Known** ▪ Privileges Language of Classroom Community ▪ Accountability to Classmates	**Distant and Other: Unknown** ▪ Privileges Language of Critical Audiences ▪ Accountability to Public
Genre	▪ Journals ▪ Diaries ▪ Logs ▪ Notebooks ▪ Freewrites ▪ Braindumps ▪ Fridgenotes ▪ Post-it Notes ▪ Weblogs (blogs)	▪ Letters ▪ Notes ▪ Questions ▪ Poems ▪ Parodies ▪ E-mail ▪ Presentation Software ▪ Web Discussion Boards	▪ Essays ▪ Articles ▪ Reports ▪ Presentation Software ▪ Memos ▪ Multimedia ▪ Web Publications
Response Time	**Immediate:** Shaping at Point of Utterance	**Quick:** from "Real" Audience—Visible and Tactile	**Lengthy:** to Publication or Presentation
	Classroom Environment ▪ Social and Collaborative ▪ Respects Diversity and Risk Taking ▪ Active Learning and Interactive Teaching ▪ Motivation for Reading and Writing		
	Developing Knowledge That Is Personally and Professionally Useful		

This chart suggests the fertile ground for the development of an interactive discourse that lies between personal discourse and public discourse. On the left side of the chart, personal discourse exhibits the familiar characteristics of informal, expressive writing. This is the discovery writing writers do for themselves in such places as journals and notebooks. On the right side, public writing exhibits the familiar characteristics of transactional, formal writing, often composed in the form of essays and reports written to a distant audience. In college classrooms, public discourse is often referred to as academic discourse, the language of the academy, or more specifically, the language of the intended audience, for example, the discourse of physics or the discourse of political science. In fact, a generally agreed upon goal for most college composition courses is to teach students to write academic discourse. One challenge for a student is to figure out how to write like an academic, or like a physicist or a political scientist, before actually becoming an academic or a physicist, that is, before knowing what a physicist knows and before acquiring the habits of mind and discourse conventions of physics that comes with knowledge and experience in that discipline. Such a rhetorical situation sometimes leads students to "fake" writing like an academic and thereby produce texts that teachers over the years have referred to as dummy runs, pretend writing, or Engfish.

This chart visualizes in the center column the actual and virtual space of the classroom, the "middle ground," where students gain knowledge, develop scholarly habits of mind, and acquire rhetorical and communication competence in a variety of public and academic contexts. It is that interactive social space where writers can combine their existing knowledge of content and inquiry with the new knowledge and experience they are acquiring in a particular course to generate texts for a "real" audience of classmates. In the process of such an interchange, knowledge is generated collaboratively and a discourse is created that is in some ways unique to those participants and that I've situated in the middle ground.

This conversational discourse of the middle ground combines the writer's existing language and rhetorical practices with those of the academy under the tutelage of the teacher, in most cases the more experienced academic practitioner. The goal becomes communicating within the context of a novice writing to a known "real" audience of other learners on or off line rather than pretending to know and thereby pretending to communicate. Examples of such writing in this booklet are the note exchange between Bill and Terry about circuit analysis (21-22), and the letter exchange between Alyson and Emily (27-28) about *Heart of Darkness*. ECAC suggests that such learning conversations can be conducted online as well as with paper and pen and with the added possibility of expanding the classroom over greater distances as well as giving students access to more written conversations and therefore more ideas and more possibilities for effective communication. Electronic media also allow such expanded communication as publication on the World Wide Web and enhancement of text with sound, color, graphics, and video.

I want to emphasize that this chart on "Classroom Discourse and Communication Across the Curriculum" is speculative and dynamic. Most genres can fall in any column or between columns or in more than one column. Email or poems or essays or letters can be written to fulfill any of the three

36

purposes or a combination. All writing, in some sense, is personal, and all writing, when read by others, is public. Further, the chart suggests that ECAC does not create new rhetorical forms nor represent a major paradigm shift, but rather represents a useful way to view written, oral, and visual language in both traditional and computer classrooms. This visualization assists me in "reading" student writing in the context of "conversational learning"—what many of us are doing for the first time with the advent of the email, computer conferencing, and the World Wide Web. Also, this chart suggests a powerful pedagogy for the development of students' language and critical thinking abilities. This chart formulates for teachers and students a recursive and dialectical language process in which the cognitive and social inform each other in the development of writers and thinkers. It helps me understand and apply the learning that occurs as teachers across the nation experiment with ECAC activities in courses within and across disciplines.

Teachers are discovering or rediscovering "middle-ground" pedagogy as they implement writing assignments that use new technologies to aid student learning and to improve communication with their students and among students in their classes. ECAC class-based projects, often developed by faculty familiar with WAC principles, incorporate various informal and formal writings and are intended for a variety of audiences: the teacher, other students, other classrooms or communities, or world-wide publication on the Web.

Email Message Exchanges

Holly Miller, a former English graduate teaching assistant at Clemson University, was a student recently in my graduate seminar in Victorian poetry. As part of our discussion of issues relating to literary study, we read Gerald Graff's *Beyond the Culture Wars: How Teaching the Conflicts Can Revitalize American Education* (Norton, 1992). In this book, Graff discusses literary canon formation, ways of "teaching the conflicts," and the role of academic discourse in constructing arguments and thereby entering the academic conversation. For her term project in my course, Holly designed an email exchange between students in her first-year composition course and graduate students enrolled in Graff's English methods course at the University of Chicago. Students were asked to read Dale Spender's "Talking in Class" (in *The Shape of Reason* by John T. Gage, Macmillan, 1991), and give their opinions on the issues raised by Spender's essay and to raise further questions that would provide an invitation and a context for Graff's students to respond to them via email and continue the conversation. Copies of all correspondence were also sent to Holly. In an earlier in-class freewrite, Holly speculated that she would be interested "in seeing how my students would respond if they had a different audience. In other words, it seems that having only me as their audience, or a 'grade-giver,' may affect the way that they respond. Maybe if they were writing to a different audience, either other students or each other, they may feel more 'passionately' about the conflicts we are exploring in 102." In response to Holly's assignment, one student wrote online the following message:

Dear Students,

Spender talks about the myth that women are the more talkative sex, but research shows that men actually talk more. So, why is this? Spender thinks it is because in our society we are still male dominated, and we encourage males to talk more than females. This encouragement starts before they even enter school. For some reason boys who talk a lot in class are thought to be bright, but girls who do the same are loud and aggressive....So how do we get girls to talk more in class? Is single-sex schools the answer? Many people think that single-sex schools is just putting off interaction with males and shelters girls from the real world.

I remember many times in elementary school not asking questions in class or answering questions....When I talked I thought I was saying something stupid and when I didn't say anything I felt stupid for not saying anything. So, to talk or not to talk is a double-edged sword for girls when it comes to talking in class....

Sincerely,

Nicole

In order to see the contrasting views that existed within the class, I'll include an example from another of Holly's students:

Dear Students,

I would like to respond to the simple question of classroom discourse as it relates to gender roles and the issues discussed. Dale Spender discusses in her absurdly inaccurate essay that women face a major dilemma in today's academic circles. She explains that a woman's amount of talk is measured against total silence. Thus woman take a secondary role in discussions, or are looked at as pushy and aggressive. She also discusses that since males dominate discussions the curriculum is molded to fit a male learning style....

....I do not believe that there is any difference between women and men in the classroom anymore....How can the classroom environment be without gender roles when the nation has many gender issues to deal with? Is it not stereotypical to group all women in the 'passive, quiet, and subservient' roles? Does this stereotype not assist the apparent problem in the classrooms if read over and over by females?

Sincerely,

Don

In her analysis of her students' e-mail messages, Holly notes the gender differences in her students' responses—that many of "the women in my class were concerned with why women don't talk in class discussions," and that the "males in my class were much more defensive in their letters, which led me to believe that they, too, are concerned with the problem and fear being included in the male stereotypes we read about." She also claims that her students' writing "became more opinionated, aggressive, and expressive."

The circumstances for the writing have changed, and Holly's students know it. They are about to discover from an interested but distant audience the value of their participation in an academic conversation, the problematizing of truths they perhaps took for granted, the kinds of evidence readers need in order to be persuaded by their general and particular assertions, the implications others see regarding gender conflicts in the classroom, and the probing social interaction that can lead to further reflection, inquiry, analysis, research, and communication. The ECAC context, in this case an email exchange of messages about an academic subject between students in very different educational situations, creates a "middle ground" between informal writing based mostly on personal experience and formal writing based primarily on substantial academic expertise. Experiences in this middle ground offer opportunities to grow as learners and as communicators. In the cases of Nicole and Don, the focus on their individual messages is central. Because Nicole's and Don's opinions, claims, personal experiences, and questions are so different, the response they receive from a reader will also be quite different—it will be a personal response to Nicole (or Don) tailored to engage her in a conversation about her ideas and concerns. However, the response will also be in an academic context shaped by the reading of Dale Spender's essay and by the knowledge and experience of her individual responder, as well as by the academic experiences of the two classes—one at Clemson and one at Chicago, and other variables that will emerge as the conversation continues. Nicole and Don will have entered an academic conversation and, like all novices, they have more to learn—about gender conflicts, about argumentation, about critical thinking, about audience analysis—but like those already in the conversation, they will be learning by doing.

Discussion Boards

In the spring of 2004, I collaborated with Magnus Gustafsson of Chalmers University in Gothenburg, Sweden, and Donna Reiss, then of Tidewater Community College in Virginia, to develop an online discussion of English translations of Swedish poetry. Students taking First-Year Composition at Tidewater Community College, Victorian Literature at Clemson University, and Fiction for Engineers at Chalmers University of Technology discussed in long online letters, using a Web discussion board, the language of these poems and the ways that readers' understanding of literary works is affected by their responses to individual words and phrases as well as the rhythms in English and Swedish of Tomas Tranströmer's poems. By writing about the poems in English, students in all three classes gained insight into the way their cultural experiences and understanding of literal and figurative meanings of words affected their understanding of the poems. Students discussed the poems and translations in groups of nine or ten. (This discussion of the Tranströmer project is part of a forthcoming book chapter "Computer-mediated Communication and the Confluence of Composition and Literature" by Katherine Fischer, Donna Reiss, and me, Art Young: NCTE, 2006).

Although only one of these classes was a writing course, all three groups of students were attentive to their own writing, to the audiences reading their prose, and to the writing choices of poets and translators. Below are excerpts from one group's discussion of Tranströmer's poem "Breathing Room: July." Wayne

39

from Tidewater noticed immediately that each translation created a different reading experience.

> The multiple translations of this poem definitely changed the imagery that the original poem had....Another example can be found in line ten of the poem. The last word of the phrase in May Swenson's translation is "lights," in Robert Fulton's translation is "straits," and in Robert Bly's translation is "bays." The three words are not synonymous and give a completely different description by that one word change in the three translations. The distinctions amongst the translations can confuse and mislead the reader into directions the poem wasn't intended to "take" the reader.

Adrian, from Chalmers and fluent in Swedish, wrote that all of the translators had changed the tone of the poem, which he perceived as calm and peaceful, with one simple word choice.

> Something that disturbs me in all of the translations is the use of the word moth as a translation to *nattfjäril*. Maybe there is no such word as "night butterfly" in English, but I think that would give a more accurate translation in aspect to the overall mood of the poem. I don't know how you react, but I definitely don't get a pleasant image on my retina when I read the words "crawl like huge moths".

Karen from Clemson in South Carolina picked up the threads begun in Virginia and Gothenburg:

> Dear Online Classmates, I have to agree with Wayne that even slightly different word choices in translation (or in the original for that matter) can confuse and mislead the reader....I especially appreciated the letter from Adrian Sparrenborn; I, too, felt the "harmony" between the man lying under the branches and the branches/tree/world....I also felt the Robert Bly translation was a little jarring, but I can't explain why. I especially appreciate the reference to the "night butterfly." There is no similar word in English; unfortunately, "moth" doesn't have quite the same poetic softness and luminary quality. The night butterfly imagery, especially coupled with "hela natten / entire night," changes the whole feel of the last stanza.

This sequence of letters demonstrates that writing to each other online fostered the very actions we encourage from writing and literature students: close attention to diction and awareness of audience. References by name to other students' posts are a clear indication that these online letters are being read and taken seriously.

Continuing the online conversation, Denise from Tidewater used Robert Bly's translation, the one Karen described as "jarring," to produce what to the others was a surprising and "jarring" interpretation, since most students saw the mood of the poem as peaceful or laid-back.

> Dear Fellow Poetry Students ....The first individual seems to be a "busy body" who even when relaxed in body, his mind "branches out in thousands of tiny branches". Seemingly, spreading himself so thin that he doesn't even realize that he has been shot right past life like a "catapult that hurls forward in slow motion."

> The second man is gazing out of the water in a world of his own. He is a man with the weight of the world on his shoulders. He grows older by the minute like the

40

docks that he stands on, "They have silver-gray posts and boulders in their gut." The worry ages him faster than necessary. The line "The dazzling light drives straight in" demonstrated that he is so engulfed in his worries that even the brightest light cannot penetrate his thought. He is lost in the ebb and tide of his life forgetting to actually live for the day.

The third man "spends the whole day in an open boat moving over the luminous bays" is living an image of relaxation and peace. However, in this illusion he simply falls asleep and lets life pass him by. He hides behind the walls of his home, "inside the shade of his blue lamp" and the events of his life "crawl like huge moths over the globe".

Then from Sweden, Sandra wrote:

As for "Breathing Space July" I think it was very exciting to read Denise's interpretation of it based on the translation by Robert Bly. I always found that one to be the harshest of them all and consequently the one furthest from how I perceived the original but Denise's letter made me realise why. That he uses "The man who" makes it into three stories about three different men, and with the use of several distressing words and phrases he makes them restless and unhappy.

"Branches out into..." results in a feeling of someone splitting his attention, desperately trying to keep track of everything, whereas "rills out..." creates a picture of someone floating into the tree and becoming a part of it in a sense....And let's not forget the disaster with the moths - as Adrian said, it really is a shame that you don't have a word like "night butterfly". Maybe one would simply have to pick an entirely different insect that could communicate the same feeling - perhaps firefly is better. What does that convey to you?

My impression on reading the Swedish version is that of the forever longed for Swedish summer. That time of the year when life seems to slow down and offer a chance to live and breathe. I also read into it the longing to return to nature. To lie beneath the trees, to stand by the lake, to sail all night - all these things represent freedom to me. It is funny to see how Bly seems to have interpreted it as more or less the opposite. I think it goes to show how much power the reader still has. I think Wayne is right in saying that it is best to read a poem in it's original format, at least if you want to be sure you have read what the poet intended, but unfortunately that isn't possible very often.

And Adrian from Chalmers also reevaluates his interpretation, and thanks to Denise and Sandra, he suggests a fuller understanding of his reading experience and a better understanding of Robert Bly's translation and interpretation—albeit not an interpretation he finally endorses.

Dear Electronic Classmates.…I found it very interesting to read Denise's interpretation of "Breathing Room: July," which differed quite much from my own. When I think back on my original perspective on the poem I thought more of the feeling that it conveyed to me, rather than searching for a more specific meaning in the words. Denise thinks of the first individual as a "busy body" who doesn't even realize that he has been "shot right past life." This is not how I imagined it, but this interpretation gives a completely new (and quite interesting, if I might add) interpretation of the poem, one that tells us not to waste our lives and enjoy every day we are alive. However, I'm not sure if that is the meaning the writer wanted to convey to us. Now that I have read the poem again, I think the writer wanted to say that we should take a break from our hectic lives and take the time to lie under the trees or sit by the docks and relax. The title "Andrum: Juli / Breathing Room: July" also seems to hint that one should take a breather.

As a few people already have I must also agree with Wayne on the translation subject. I think that Wayne makes a very good point when he writes: "A translation can change everything about the original poem." This is something that we have all experienced from the various translations of "Andrum: Juli."

Karen from Clemson then described a "cultural" reading that might have influenced the different ways readers in Sweden and readers in the southern U.S. were experiencing the poem.

I wanted to comment on the Breathing Room: July comments. Thank you especially to Cheryl and Sandra for you references to slowing down and basking. I failed to see that when I initially read the interpretations. Sandra's remarks about the "forever longed for Swedish summer" helped put it in perspective. With the very mild winters and the summer heat and humidity we have here in South Carolina (and in tidewater Virginia as well), I failed to see the appeal that July would have in Sweden. For those of us that don't like the oppressive heat, "July" hardly evokes a time when we could slow down and breathe easy. This only serves to illustrate that not only the author's context, but the reader's context, will affect the interpretation of a work.

Until next time, Karen

These excerpts from a much longer epistolary conversation that took place over two weeks in Spring 2004 demonstrate an interactive critical engagement with literature and with diverse readers of literature that can't be reproduced in a traditional classroom. The Internet enabled our students to cross geographical and intellectual boundaries and to write insightfully, collaboratively, and effectively for engaged readers who take their words and thoughts seriously. Although students were assigned deadlines for their responses to the poems and each other, asynchronicity allowed them to read and write in their own time and in their own time zones.

Not to be underestimated in projects like this one is the value of collaboration among colleagues working in different institutions, states, and countries. All assignment design, like the students' letters, was asynchronous, using email to discuss topics and approaches that would be sensitive to their varied experience writing about literature, writing online, and writing in English. With the advent of free Internet telephoning, we now also communicate orally across the web and the globe. All three teachers ended the assignment with enthusiasm for the ways in which students embraced this activity. This project, entitled "Cross-Cultural Collaboration Among Swedish and American Students," is online at <http://wordsworth2.net/projects/crossculturalcollabs/>.

Guidelines for Designing Electronic Discussions

In electronic environments, responses to ideas and texts are dialogic rather than solitary and foster ongoing written conversations among readings and readers. These guidelines should be adapted to course content, design, and emphasis, as well as to the type of electronic communication (email list, discussion board, or weblog, for instance). They were developed collaboratively by Katie Fischer, Donna Reiss, and Art Young.

1. Carefully integrate electronic discussions into course goals, not as add-on assignments. Participation should be mandatory, and on-time participation is crucial to establishing a conversational, academic exchange.
2. Give students credit for engaged participation, but not necessarily grades. Respond encouragingly to insightful posts to provide students with models for a successful exchange.
3. Offer precise directions with clear expectations: scope, approach, tone (courteous and respectful of various viewpoints), length (minimum and maximum—we recommend 250-350 words), diction (such as "edited conversational"), form or genre (letter or memo or report).
4. Consider integrating Internet research, in which students include relevant Web addresses as active links in their messages to each other, for example, a Web page from an engineering research Weblog, an article in a discipline-specific online journal, or a Pre-Raphaelite painting from The Victorian Web. When appropriate, encourage students to incorporate visual images and multimedia.
5. Encourage explanations, examples, questions, speculations, alternative viewpoints, and connections to personal experience.
6. Develop topics and assignments that will elicit engagement with course material as well as the answers and responses you seek. Sometimes you'll want to be quite specific about topics and approaches; sometimes you'll want to be more open-ended, allowing the first person who posts to determine the topic and approach.
7. Encourage or require students to quote from course materials and texts and from their classmates' posts when they respond to each other within groups and when they write tests or essays on the topics they discussed online.
8. Have students include their own and one or more classmates' posts in their final course portfolios along with a reflection on what was learned from the e-discussion process.
9. Assign small groups, for example, five-to-seven students who read and respond to each other. Every group's posts should be available to the whole class, but students need only read their own group's writing.
10. Develop a heuristic. For example, here's an adaptable approach that can be made more fluid or more directive.
    a. First post: Respond to the reading or assigned topic with specific reference to the reading. Include a brief summary, select a specific

        focus or point, develop that point with explanations and examples, and invite commentary from classmates about a particular concern, not the whole post, ending with an invitation or question.

b.   Second post: Read all the posts in your group and then respond to the first post of a classmate who has not yet received a reply. Include specific reference to the main idea of the classmate's post and to the assigned topic, expand on the classmate's ideas with additional information or ideas or offer an alternative viewpoint on the topic. Support your position with references to the reading or posts by other group members. Perhaps raise questions and speculate further on the topic.

c.   Third post: Respond to the person who answered your first post with appreciation for their response and an explanation of ways their message increased your own understanding or stimulated your thinking. Remember your audience is a specific individual plus your whole class.

d.   Additional post: Summarize all the messages from your group and analyze for primary points, similarities and differences, and other observations about the group's thinking.

e.   Additional post: For a subsequent post, respond to one or more classmates from a different group than the one you have been participating in.

f.   If the class meets in person, gather the writing group to discuss the issues in person and report orally to the class as a whole.

Reflective Writing

At the completion of a communication task, whether written, oral, visual, digital, or multi-modal, an important piece of writing that students can do is a "reflection." At the conclusion of her graduate seminar, Holly Miller (37-39) wrote a reflective introduction to introduce her portfolio of work produced over the course of the term. About her term project she wrote, in part:

> I never realized how much of a difference audiences make in getting students to respond. I learned this not only in my own letter writing with group members in Victorian Poetry, but also in reading the email letters of my own students to Dr. Graff's students. Never before in graduate school have I felt like I was learning as much as I was teaching....The letter writing gave me a chance to think about a classmate's questions and concerns, while giving me enough time to articulate a response that I felt well-formed. And, in writing my own response, it made me really think about what I was saying so that others could understand. In addition, having to formulate my own thoughts in writing sparked many more questions than if I had just responded 'off the top of my head' in class, or just taken notes on the subject. It created a dialogue that carried outside the classroom, and I saw the advantages of this mostly in my own students' writing.

Holly has mined the middle ground of academic language for the possibilities of interactive writing and conversational learning to enhance her teaching and her learning and that of her students. She too is learning by doing.

I'll cite one other example of reflective writing, the kind of writing we do when we carefully consider our learning, our thinking, and the' applications of what we are learning to other areas of our lives (for an example of a reflection from an electrical engineering class, see Susan's note to Mr. McAuliff, 24-26). In Fall 2004, a class of future secondary teachers at Clemson enrolled in my senior-level "Composition for Teachers." As part of their course requirements they participated in a blog electronic discussion with D. W. Daniel High School students enrolled in Nancy Swanson's Advanced Placement English class. Students read Tim O'Brien's novel, *The Things They Carried,* about the Vietnam War, and students wrote, posted, and responded to blog letters within groups composed of correspondents from both classes. They explored together the experience of the novel and the insights, connections, and questions it raised for them about numerous social issues, such as war, peace, gender, culture, family, and the draft, as well as literary issues such as the author's intention, the nature of fiction, character motivation, textual evidence, and their own voices as writers.

At the conclusion of two weeks of this blogging project and writing four posts and reading about thirty posts, Clemson student Patrick wrote, in part, this reflection about the experience:

> ...I liked the blog and how I could enter and edit my comment without outside interruption. Sometimes I get lost in class discussion: thoughts are being expressed, opinions are spouted, and topics are jumping from one to the next. I often think of something to put into the discussion and lose my train of thought while someone else is speaking. Or, I second-guess myself if someone else says something contradictory to what I'm thinking. Being able to write in the blog let me share my points without interruption and without hearing others' varying opinions while I am trying to form my own thoughts. It made my writing a little stronger, too, because I had the information from the text there in front of me, and I had the time to search for passages to back up what I was saying. The blog gave me time to express those ideas and revise my points before putting them out there for others' scrutiny. I tried to carry this process over to the class discussions, but it often didn't work.

In his reflection, written to his teacher and, in this case, not posted for others to read, Patrick recounts his experience of writing the blog entries, and he compares this online asynchronous discussion to face-to-face class discussion. He recounts the interactive process he has gone through—interactive with texts and other readers—and he describes how he tries to make his contribution persuasive to others. Interestingly, Patrick tries to adapt the same process to oral conversation, but "it often didn't work." Patrick is discovering for himself part of the value of written conversation, with its time for thinking, for revising, and for gathering evidence "without interruption" to make his "writing a little stronger," and he also realizes that part of the value of classroom conversation is its immediacy and rapid accumulation of common references and diverse opinions. Both written and oral conversation with an engaged audience about academic topics leads to learning (about the novel, about the Vietnam War, about a range of political perspectives), but Patrick's written reflection primarily assists him in learning how to learn and how to apply learning to new situations.

Reflections can be written at any point in a course: after students have read a book chapter, turned in a test, written a poem, or solved a calculus problem.

They can be written in class in five minutes or out of class, over a longer period, as a careful and thoughtful reflection on an entire semester's work and learning. They are of value to writers who desire to review, synthesize, analyze, organize, and contextualize the knowledge they have gained. They are of value to teachers who want to know more about how students learn and desire to maintain regular student-teacher communication about what students know and what they believe they should be learning, what they are actually learning, and why, and how.

■Chapter 4: Writing To Communicate

As we consider further how to assist students in developing their writing abilities, we can construct assignments and classroom practices that focus on writing to communicate, that focus on the right side of my "Writing and Thinking" chart on page 9 and the right side of my "Classroom Discourse and Communication Across the Curriculum" chart on page 35. And even though these charts divide classroom writing into distinct categories, I want to emphasize the common connections and interrelationships between writing to learn and writing to communicate. In both kinds of writing, students need to be actively involved in thinking and solving problems, in developing knowledge and applications of it. Or to look at this learning situation from another angle, writing assignments should not have as their primary purpose to "test" students' knowledge of textbook or lecture material, situations in which the teacher knows the right answer and is just checking to see if the students know it too. People most often write to communicate information, perspectives, or experiences to an audience that will find in the writing something new. Teachers are not eager readers when they must read numerous student essays or reports in which they don't expect to learn anything new, and students (or anyone else) are not eager writers when they write for readers who already know everything they have to say. Teachers, of course, often expect to test students' knowledge of textbook and lecture material, and I am not arguing against doing so. What I am suggesting is that teachers separate the testing function from the communication function in designing assignments and that assignments designed to develop students' communication abilities as well as their knowledge and understanding of course material be ones in which the writer is involved in a real communication situation—when knowledge is passed from someone who has it to someone who doesn't have it—rather than a testing situation.

Often we feel that communication skills can be taught in a vacuum, independent of a person's knowledge of a particular subject or understanding of the rhetorical context. But writing across the curriculum addresses the issue of improving students' written communication abilities by saying that learning to write effectively is dependent on the students' knowledge of the subject matter as well as their understanding of the social context for the writing. Thus WAC has gained many adherents in all disciplines because it sees mastery of knowledge and its applications as central to becoming an effective practitioner and communicator within any discipline. For example, a geology professor in teaching students the knowledge that is geology as well as how to think, communicate, and solve problems like a geologist is initiating students into geology as a discipline and into science as a profession. Sometimes teachers fear that becoming involved in WAC means taking time away from geology— becoming an English teacher for 30 percent of the time—and they are understandably reluctant to do so. WAC says that a geology professor should not attempt to become an English professor at all. Geologists should teach geology, its knowledge and its ways of developing and communicating knowledge, and they should utilize written language as a tool to strengthen this teaching and learning of geology.

So writing-to-communicate assignments should be designed to expand and refine students' knowledge and mastery of the subject matter—a goal they share with writing-to-learn assignments. But writing to communicate differs from writing to learn in that emphasis is placed on communicating that learning to others in the most effective way the circumstances allow. Emphasis is placed on distant audiences, on discourse forms, on clarity and precision in thought and style, on sincerity and authority, on constructing texts that increase the chances that what the writer has to say will be heard. It assumes that the writer has something he or she wants to say as well as readers who want to hear it. And this is one recursive link to writing to learn—for in writing to learn writers often develop a better understanding of the subject and discover what it is they have to say about it, a process we saw at work in the notebook of Thomas Edison on pages 12-13. The writer, having explained the matter to himself or herself, now may face the challenge of explaining the matter to others. And we can help writers learn to write in ways that increase the chances of their ideas and opinions being taken seriously.

The issue of sincerity is a key one. When writers write creatively, we give them their "fictions," we understand they are "making up" facts or characters in order to see things anew or things that never were. When writers write to learn we know they are not concerned about whether readers understand or believe them, because they are writing to work things out for themselves, they are trying to make discoveries, and they can't guarantee that discoveries will be made. But when writers write to inform or persuade us, when they seek to communicate information that they say will be important to us, then readers have the right to expect that the writers have done their homework, know what they are talking about, have organized their information meaningfully and efficiently, and are telling the truth as they see it.

For teachers, then, one important issue is to design assignments in which students can generate meaningful and sincere communication for readers who will find it useful. Although teachers do not intend to do so, we often create writing assignments that put students in the position of "faking it"—faking that they have more knowledge than they do, faking that they have more authority than they do, faking that they have something important to say, faking that they believe there are readers who really want to read what they write. When we design such assignments, we receive numerous essays or reports in which students practice at thinking and communicating, go through the motions, rather than actually think and communicate. When we read such writing, we are disappointed for many reasons, but one important reason is that the trust between reader and writer has been broken; there has not been a sincere attempt to communicate. While we should not feel responsible every time a student attempts to "fake it," we should realize that when students fail to fulfill our expectations for their writing, we may unwittingly be encouraging such behavior through our assignments and classroom practices. For example, we should not assign students to write "practice" memos of no real interest to readers because someday when they are in industry they will have to write memos. If we assign memos, we should do so because writing them will contribute to the generation and communication of knowledge and its applications important to course goals.

This was the kind of thinking that led me to design the letter exchange in my Victorian literature class (pages 27-30). While I originally conceived of it as a writing-to-learn assignment, I now see it as somewhere in between writing to learn and writing to communicate, in what I call "the middle ground" of conversational learning. From reading these student letters, I learned much that is useful to me about using writing to communicate in my classes. In their response to a classmate's letter of inquiry, I required that students type the letter, that it be longer than the first letter, and that it include references to primary and secondary sources. But I maintained more informal aspects such as the form of the personal letter (rather than the critical essay) and the less threatening and more authentic audience of a fellow student. As a secondary audience, I read these letters in my teacher-as-mentor role, looking to see what discoveries and problems these letters uncovered, rather than reading them in my teacher-as-evaluator role, examining each one for how well it fulfilled my expectations of formal, publishable literary criticism (or, to tell the truth, how far short it fell of those expectations). In reading Alyson's and the other students' letters, I realized that they did not have to "fake" knowledge and expertise they did not have, that these letters were sincere and truthful in ways these same students' critical essays were not. After only a week studying this novel, my students and I were not prepared to write a publishable essay, although we could have pretended that we were and practiced writing one. But after only a week of study, my students had generated important insights about *Heart of Darkness* and sincere reactions to the many troubling themes within the novel. They were prepared to write a letter to a classmate in response to specific questions about their common experience of reading, studying, and talking about the novel over a week's time, to a classmate who asked difficult questions but who also understood the time frame and context in which the response was generated. I'm convinced that these letters contributed significantly to my students' ability to read literature, to interpret *Heart of Darkness*, and to develop the language and thinking abilities to write sincerely about literature. One ongoing task, which I hope you will share with me, is to develop writing-to-communicate assignments and classroom practices that encourage sincere and authentic communication. What follows is some of my current thinking about writing to communicate—thinking that has been shaped over the years by my collaboration with faculty in nearly every discipline.

Time and Process

Most of us are familiar with the traditional way of assigning an important paper in a class—we've experienced it many times as students, even if we haven't assigned it as teachers. Such assigned papers are included on the course syllabus and mentioned on the first day of class so students can arrange their time to work on them throughout the course, and they are due near the end of the course. Guidelines are usually included on the syllabus as well: approved subjects for research and writing, minimum number of words or pages, number of secondary sources, and so on. The teacher may remind students again about two weeks before they are due, because he or she realizes that some may need such a reminder. The papers are then collected on the due date, graded, sometimes with critical and encouraging comments, and returned on the last day of class. If students are absent that day, they likely will never pick up their papers. In addition to providing a rationale for the grade assigned, the comments are meant to help the students improve their writing the next time they write a paper in another course, in another discipline, in another term.

Writing across the curriculum draws on recent research from composition studies to suggest ways to make such writing assignments more meaningful for teachers and students alike. Teachers can work to integrate such assignments into the learning of the course by focusing time and attention on the writing process. We know ourselves, as researchers, that we usually cannot write a successful refereed article in a weekend, even on a topic we've studied for some time; and yet undergraduate students, faced with unfamiliar subjects and unfamiliar contexts for writing about those subjects, often find themselves having to write a paper under those conditions. By slowing down the process and occasionally intervening in it, teachers can create an environment with time both for learning and for improving communication.

"Could Artificial Intelligence Get Out of Hand?": An Example

The following selection is from a formal essay written by a student in the Computers and Society course conducted in the mid 1980s. In this course, students studied the social and ethical implications of computers and were required to write a seven-to-ten page essay, informed by library research, on relevant topics. The essay was assigned about halfway through the course and was due a month later. Because his father had lost his job at General Motors in the early 1980s when the industry increased the use of robots in assembly, Ed chose to write on the topic of "AI unemployment." I quote two selections from his essay: the introduction and the conclusion.

Could Artificial Intelligence Get Out of Hand?

The idea of Artificial Intelligence (AI) as an advancement in computer technology has been around since the late 50s and early 60s, but in just the last few years, some critics have begun to pose the question, "What about AI unemployment"? There is much disagreement on the answer to this question among authorities on the subject. Some consider AI to be a boon to the economics of the future, while others view it as a threat to man's existence. It is these differences in opinion that I wish to explore, discuss, and form them to make a clear and logical and hopefully favorable approach to Artificial Intelligence.

A large part of the advancement in AI research is in the field of robotics. This is all very promising to robotics engineers, but what about the inevitable drastic replacement of human labor?

According to Ira Pohl (259) there are currently about 25 million Americans employed as manufacturers. Marc Leepson (125) cites that (as of 1981) there are 3,800 robots working in American factories alone. But with such high production rates from robots, five dollars per hour as compared to twelve to twenty dollars per hour for the same job done by a human, what company can resist (Pohl, 291). I fear an imminent danger of us "technologizing" ourselves right out of worthwhile existence.

A vast majority of the world's large corporations are or are soon going to be switching most of their assembly lines over to robotics. General Electric Corp. has plans to replace over half of its 37,000 manufacturers with robots. Some of the assembly workers will be given new jobs, but obviously most will be laid off (Leepson, 127). . .

       *   *   *   *

Despite all science fiction speculations of the past few decades, the vast majority of AI writers and researchers continue to highly praise its capabilities. AI programs are already in small scale use in many fields, including farming, mining, manufacturing, schools and hospitals (Winston, 2). The computer now has the ability to diagram complex chemical structures faster than any analytical chemist around through a program called "Dendral" (Schaffer, 14).

So it seems that computers are making astonishing progress in automating the thinking and manufacturing world of today. AI programming can lower the cost of production—and simultaneously raise the quality—of goods and services that we buy (Nilsson, 27).

In conclusion, I feel that my viewpoint on AI has drastically changed as I have written this paper. I started out toying with the idea of a radical, computer-controlled totalitarian society and have ended up "realizing" that AI really does have the potential to make our lives easier and more productive. In the process, I originally started out trying to deal with the dangers of "AI unemployment" but I then realized that in the opinions of the technical world, this is not a worrisome concern. Also, because of a lack of research materials on the subject, I had to leave the idea as a question for the reader to answer for him or herself. Therefore, I have, like I said, come to realize the many benefits of continued research in Artificial Intelligence and have enjoyed writing this paper as a learning experience.

    I want to examine what Ed has written in some detail, and then I want to suggest classroom practices that may have helped Ed further his understanding of the social implications of artificial intelligence and the effectiveness of his essay. In so doing, we will look at "what is going on" in Ed's essay as well as suggest ways teachers might intervene to good effect in the learning process.

    When I conduct a faculty workshop using Ed's writing as a sample of writing to communicate, I often follow the same procedure as I did for the writing-to-learn example, "My Utopia" (pages 5-8). Participants make lists of perceived strengths and weaknesses, construct ways of using such writing in class, suggest ways of responding to and evaluating Ed's writing. There is usually general agreement that, as a college sophomore, Ed is an intelligent and articulate thinker and writer but that he still has a lot to learn about both the social implications of AI and about how to construct an effective essay that is both informative and persuasive. As teachers, we want to help Ed mature as a thinker and writer, so let us begin by reading his essay again. And as we do, I'll give you an interpretation of Ed's essay based on my distinction between writing to learn and writing to communicate.

    As I read Ed's first paragraph, I note that he is familiar with this kind of writing. He poses a question, one he suggests has become important "in just the last few years." He goes on to say that there is much disagreement between critics and "authorities" on this issue. Then he informs the reader what he intends to do: review the research related to "these differences in opinion" and form them into "a clear and logical" statement so the reader can benefit from Ed's knowledge of this increasingly important topic. In the abstract, this might be considered a textbook example of how to write an introduction to an academic essay.

I also note other things as I read Ed's first paragraph. He characterizes all the authorities as "either/or" on the issue of artificial intelligence (AI). It is either a "boon" or a "threat," and I wonder if Ed's thinking will continue in the either/or pattern. Such a pattern is sometimes labeled "dualistic" thinking, in which a person sees only the good or the bad side of an issue and is not prepared to deal with degrees of complexity and various shades of ambiguity. I wonder at the word "hopefully" and its placement within the last sentence. What does he mean by a "hopefully favorable approach" to AI? Is he saying that he wants his report to show AI in a favorable light—that he will take the "boon" side of the debate? Or is he saying that he himself doesn't yet know the results of his investigation—his exploring, discussing, forming—and that when he is done he *hopes* his statement is clear and logical? Or is he not quite sure what he is saying? This "hopefully" combined with other evidence indicates to me that Ed may be writing a "discovery draft." Ed is writing to figure out what he thinks about this subject—and he will let the reader follow this process. But the reader expects a writing-to-communicate draft—the reader wants to know what Ed thinks after he has made his discoveries, gone down the blind alleys, synthesized and analyzed the research.

In his second through fourth paragraphs Ed further defines and limits his topic to "robotics," asks another key question ("but what about the inevitable drastic replacement of human labor?"), cites compelling evidence from Pohl and Leepson, and suggests an answer—we are in "imminent danger." He contrasts the engineers and companies who have much to gain from robotics research and its transfer to the workplace and the "assembly workers" who have much to lose. He appears sympathetic to the workers even as he realizes that robots are "inevitable" and corporations "are or are soon" going to switch.

The last sentence of the third paragraph is notable: "I fear an imminent danger of us 'technologizing' ourselves right out of worthwhile existence." He uses "I" to directly express his opinion, something he doesn't do elsewhere (until the essay's final paragraph). And because this is such a strong statement, the reader expects the rest of the essay to be an indictment of using robotics technology to replace workers. Ed is now firmly on the "threat" side of the dichotomy he set up in his first paragraph. The reader is less sure about the "favorable" of the first paragraph—it no longer seems to mean that Ed is on the "boon" side.

Now to reread the last three paragraphs, beginning with the first two of these, which I take to be the formal conclusion to his essay. Writing in an impersonal, authoritative voice (he doesn't use "I"), he concludes by coming down squarely and without question on the side of "boon." He has read many AI researchers, and this is their conclusion, and so it will be his. In fact, it appears that when he was reading Pohl and Leepson, Ed agreed with them about the "threat" of AI, but now he has read many more researchers, including Winston, Schaffer, and Nilsson, and he agrees with them about the astonishing "boon." He began by asking a question in his title—"could artificial intelligence get out of hand?"—and since his dualistic thinking has led him and us to expect a yes or no answer—the answer appears to be "no." Given the first part of his paper, the "imminent danger" he felt and wanted us to feel also, his answer surprises us. It may also be a surprise to Ed as his concluding language suggests—"So it seems that," with its implied sense of wonder at where his research journey has taken him.

I have read many student essays that have concluded in just this way. They begin in one place with one premise and conclude in quite a different place with a new premise, often one that directly contradicts where they began. I do not read such writing as a lack of intelligence or writing ability by the student, but rather as a very natural part of the writing process, although not appropriate in this context. Ed has written a writing-to-learn draft when the teacher expected a writing-to-communicate final draft. Ed is primarily explaining the matter to himself rather than explaining the matter to others. In a writing-to-learn draft, it does not matter if a writer begins one place, makes discoveries along the way, and ends up in another place. In fact, this is a good way to "explain the matter to oneself." Such writing often enables the writing and thinking process, but it is ineffective as writing to communicate. It is not sincere. Ed has committed himself to meaningfully synthesizing the relevant research and then reporting and interpreting the results to us in a "clear and logical" manner, and he has not done that. When I say this writing is not sincere, I do not mean unethical (as in deliberate lying). I simply mean it is not trustworthy or convincing. Although Ed writes with formal conventions that imply this is a final draft, not a discovery draft, that he has thought long and hard about AI unemployment, that he has himself resolved key questions, that he has knowledge and insights that will be worth our time to read, his words betray him. He is "faking it."

The most interesting thing about this essay, and the reason I chose it as my example, is that Ed is aware of this tension, aware of how he has not fulfilled reader expectations, and he writes his remarkable "In conclusion" paragraph as a way of resolving this tension. As we read this paragraph, we notice the style, tone, and audience have changed. The rest of the essay is fairly objective in style and tone—the impersonal researcher voice writing to an audience of interested professionals or to the teacher-as-evaluator. But this final paragraph is highly personal in style and tone—and written by a particular student, Ed, to a particular instructor in the teacher-as-mentor role. Ed frankly admits that his essay begins one place and ends another—that as he read more technical research during the process of drafting the essay he ended up "realizing" that his first premise was not defensible. Yet, he seems to say, with more time and access to other research materials, maybe it would be defensible. For now, readers will just have to decide for themselves whether AI is a boon or threat. He knows what the researchers have to say, but he also knows the impact of a lost job on his and other families, and he has not yet found that perspective represented in his library research. So, he seems to say to the teacher, I know I have not fulfilled your expectations for a formal research paper, but I want you to know that I have learned a lot in doing this project and that I am continuing to think about it. Writing this essay was a more important learning experience for me than what the final product demonstrates. Not surprisingly, and even though Ed may be arguing for leniency in the grading process, this final paragraph is sincere in the way the rest of his essay is not. Even though in his previous two paragraphs Ed reaches the conclusion that AI is a "boon," he confides in the last paragraph that this is not really a trustworthy conclusion. In order to reach a trustworthy conclusion, Ed seems to know he needs to do more research, needs to continue to think critically about what he knows and learns (from both his research and his personal experience), needs to think and to write in different ways.

How can we help Ed and other students in their struggle to become effective and trustworthy communicators? We'll continue to use Ed's essay as an example as we consider various classroom practices designed to assist students develop the thinking and writing abilities of successful professionals. We'll focus on using the writing process as a strategy for teaching and for learning in all disciplines.

Classroom Practices

We know there is no such thing as "the" writing process—a uniform procedure that all writers follow. Different writers use different processes, and the same writer uses different processes in different contexts. Certainly, one contextual variation in writing tasks is the amount of time available to complete the task. If a good amount of time is available and the task is a lengthy and important one, then most writers benefit from writing a draft, allowing it to sit for a while, getting suggestions from others, and then going back with fresh eyes to revise or edit. When little time is available, writers make do by developing strategies for particular contexts, as do journalists who work under same-day deadlines. Thus, in our classrooms, we should recognize similar variations, variations dependent on contextual issues such as course goals and time constraints (on both student and teacher). For example, some student writing should be revised, and some student writing, even if judged to be poorly written, should be set aside, and the class move on to new issues and new writing tasks. Ed would benefit from revising his essay following constructive feedback from the teacher and perhaps others, but he needs the time for further research, drafting, and feedback. Whether to build such time into a course for this assignment depends on the teacher's course goals. In most cases, having more time to research, reflect, resee, and revise his essay will enable Ed to learn more about the social issues of artificial intelligence, learn more about how to do research on them, learn more about how to synthesize, analyze, evaluate, and make judgments about them, and learn more about writing effectively about them. If these goals are important, then we need to slow down and intervene in the process.

So I will use a "generic" version of "the" writing process as a vehicle for discussing classroom practices. We'll consider various strategies Ed's teacher might have introduced to create a supportive environment for his growth as a thinker and writer, recognizing that teachers and students should pick and choose among strategies that best fit their purposes. For the sake of convenience, I will break down the writing process into six parts that in practice often overlap or circle back: planning, drafting (including audience-related issues), revising, editing, proofreading, and publication.

Class activities in weeks preceding the submission of a draft encourage idea generation.

- Ed could keep a journal, a notebook, or a weblog of his research notes and reflections; a double-entry notebook might be valuable—one side of the page for recording research and the other side for reflections and questions about the research.
- Ed could join with classmates in groups of five to jointly conduct research, ask questions, and report findings to each other on a listserv.
- Ed and his classmates could be led by the teacher in a brainstorming session in which they generate possible topics and characterize the possibilities and the problems of each.
- Ed could submit an outline of his essay to his teacher for suggestions and/or to peers for feedback.
- Ed could write a freewrite or post to a discussion board in which he explains what he is confident about in writing the essay and where he is having difficulties or is less confident and could use some advice.
- Ed could write a proposal to his teacher in which he states his purpose, identifies his audience, and describes and defends his organizational scheme.
- Ed could write a microtheme on an aspect of AI unemployment. A microtheme is written or typed on a 5 " x 8 " index card and demands careful planning, thinking, and organizing in a few well-chosen words.
- Ed could review and analyze professional models of essays like the one he is writing.
- Ed could write a poem on the subject of his essay (also see pages 17-20). Indeed, here is the poem Ed wrote on AI.

Artificial Intelligence

"Oh, back in the good old days,
when men were still men,"
prints a sentimental computer.

But since then things have changed.

Computers are making computers that make computers
and computers are governing other computers.
Computers are repairing other computers
and computers are preparing jobs for computers.
Computers are designing computer art
and printing computer books.

But where is man?
He sits back idly, counting the sand.
Nothing left for him to do.

But the compassionate computer commences—
Men made real art,
wrote real books,
made real jobs,
and governed with wisdom other men.

"I don't know" queries the tearful computer,
"shouldn't we risk giving their intelligence back?"

"Naaa," says a cynical counterpart,
"what if they got out of hand?"

Here is Ed's initial perception of a "radical, computer-controlled totalitarian society" (to quote from Ed's essay), depicted with irony and humor. He creates a world in which people have abdicated their thinking and working to machines, a world in which his "fear" that people will "technologize" themselves right out of a worthwhile existence has come true. Ed gives his computers personified thoughts and feelings because humans no longer have them, and he concludes with an ironic reversal of roles in which he imagines the computers debating the threat of human intelligence to machine intelligence. And in this world, cynicism wins out over sentiment, authority over empathy, just as they did in the human world of bygone days. Ed is writing science fiction, and he is imagining one possible scenario arising out of artificial intelligence. Such poems, when read by teacher and classmates, contribute to the learning and planning process: discussions can be generated around numerous issues, and distinctions can be made between writing a poetic fiction and writing an informative essay.

❑ DRAFTING

Class activities enable and support the writing of a readable draft.

- Ed could analyze models from students who wrote similar essays in previous classes—excellent, acceptable, and unacceptable ones—and then work with a group to characterize the features of each.
- Ed could review a similar essay written by the teacher, including the changes that took place between drafts. Various drafts of the essay could be posted on the class website, or posted in a course management system.
- Ed could draft the first page or two of his essay and then read it aloud to classmates in small groups and receive feedback.
- Ed should be encouraged to save and back up drafts on his computer thus making subsequent revisions easier.
- Ed could be encouraged to work on the issue of audience as he drafts.

Identifying, imagining, and visualizing an audience and a context for writing to that audience is central to the composing process. Experts disagree about at what point writers consider issues of audience, but most agree it is often early in the composing process, in planning or drafting. Researchers have also pointed out that while most professionals usually write to a variety of audiences as part of their responsibilities, students quite often go years writing to just one audience—the teacher. Writing changes in significant ways as the audience for that writing changes, and students need to experience such changes as they write in college. Ed's teacher could assign the audience for the AI essay or could let Ed develop one. But, in fact, neither the teacher nor Ed seems to have considered issues of audience—and therefore his essay lacks focus and appears to be written to different audiences in different places. It has the appearance of being written in a vacuum, without a context other than to receive a grade—an exercise in "practice" writing. Here are some options for Ed to integrate issues of audience into his draft:

- Ed could write two brief versions of his essay to different audiences: one as a letter to his father and one as a scholarly article to an AI research journal, or one as an academic essay to his classmates and one as an informative booklet for sixth-grade students. He and his classmates could notice how both content and language change depending on audience and context.

- Because a teacher may want the knowledge each student gains in individual research projects to become part of the entire class's knowledge, he or she may identify the audience as Ed's classmates (including the teacher). Thus, reading each other's writing becomes an important part of knowledge generated by the class. To enhance this process, some teachers publish student essays in print or on the web. Some teachers require oral reports. And some teachers require students to quote from one another as part of their research documentation.

- Either Ed or the teacher could identify a "real" audience beyond the classroom who would be interested in reading about such a topic: perhaps the newsletter editor at a labor union's local office or a computer science professor working on AI. Perhaps Ed could interview such people.

- Ed could role-play an audience and a motivation for writing. He is a researcher preparing a report for a lawyer suing to protect workers from being replaced by robots, or he is preparing a report for a lawyer defending a company's personnel policies.

- Ed could correspond via email with students at another college working on a similar research project.

- Ed could write to the teacher as professional evaluator, playing the role of a journal editor and making judgments on the quality of Ed's essay. This, more or less, is the traditional audience for student writing. It is an important audience, but it should not be the only audience a student writes for in two or four years of college.

❏ **REVISING**

After a draft is completed, classroom activities are supportive and critical to encourage further writing and rewriting. If a course goal is to have students improve when they write to communicate, the most efficient and productive way to guide such improvement may be to have Ed and his classmates revise their writing after receiving suggestions and criticisms from supportive readers.

- Ed could bring his draft to class and in class could write a letter to readers or a self-evaluation of his draft (see pages 61-65 following). How can readers most help him in their response? On what specific issues would he like readers to give him feedback? What is he pleased with and where does he see problems? What would he improve if he had more time for research and writing? He then would attach this to the draft to guide readers (peers and/or teacher) in assisting him with his writing.
- Ed could receive feedback from his teacher in the teacher-as-mentor role: the teacher's comments attempt to help Ed resee his writing (and not just tinker at editing it); point out strengths as well as weaknesses (suggest what Ed might build on in the next draft); focus on two or three key issues so as not to overwhelm Ed; and leave decision making to Ed rather than tell him what he must do to satisfy the teacher on the next draft.
- Ed could be asked to make an outline of his essay after he has completed the first draft to see if it coheres or consider how the organization could be improved. If Ed is having particular trouble with organization, he could write three brief alternative outlines and then consider which might be the most effective given his purpose and audience.
- Ed could be asked to write out in complete sentences the three most important things he learned in doing AI research and in writing the draft and then review if they are properly identified and featured in his draft.
- Ed could receive oral feedback about his draft from his group members, from his teacher in a conference, or from teacher and classmates in a group conference. Ed needs to know that there are readers interested in reading his next draft, readers who are eager to see what it might become. If Ed senses that this is not true, and he can't see how to make it true, he should be free to choose another topic for his next draft. Ed's readers expect him to be "sincere" in his writing, and they must be sincere in their responses during and after the drafting of the essay.
- Ed could visit the campus writing center with his draft and receive individual attention and suggestions from a trained peer tutor or a professional writing consultant.
- Ed could revise this draft in response to "provocative revision" prompts supplied by the teacher or other readers. As a way of helping Ed resee his writing, the teacher asks that the next draft include references to social science research on technology/labor issues and not just "technical" research, that it include one or more descriptive examples of people affected by AI unemployment—a worker, a worker's spouse, a manager, or someone else—and that it explore at least briefly the notion that AI may be both a boon and a threat at the same time. If Ed doesn't believe that these prompts improve his writing, he should be free to drop them from a subsequent draft. (Such provocative prompts are meant to encourage Ed to continue the learning process begun with his draft and not to regard this early draft as an almost final product that

just needs a little tinkering with spelling, punctuation, and word choice and then will be resubmitted. In other words, it is meant to encourage revision instead of editing at this stage in the essay's development.)

❑ **EDITING**

After the drafting process, after essays are as focused and organized as the situation allows, classroom practices can be designed to assist students with the editing process. Editing seeks to make writing as reader-friendly as possible without compromising the writer's rhetorical and stylistic intent. In most academic situations, reader-friendly writing observes the customs and conventions of standard English. In most cases, teachers who construct an assignment to assist students at various stages of the writing process should not respond to issues of revision and issues of editing on the same draft. They should first respond to issues of revision and only later to issues of editing. When teachers make suggestions for refining a thesis or reorganizing an essay and circle comma errors at the same time, they send a confusing message to the student writer. In revising the essay, the problem sentence might not even recur—and yet the student may feel he or she has to include it to show the teacher he has corrected the error. Thus, such mixed messages can interfere with a productive revising process.

- Ed could exchange his draft with another student to edit each other's work. Learning to critique and edit another's writing will also help Ed grow as a writer.
- Ed and his classmates could work with a Prentice Hall handbook as they edit their writing to accomplish their purposes and engage their readers.
- Ed could submit his draft to the teacher, who edits the first page or two as a model for editing for clarity, conciseness, and correctness and then returns the draft to Ed to edit the remaining pages with the same care and attention to detail.
- Ed and his classmates could work on some "generic" editing exercises but in the context of their own writing. For example, they could circle all the prepositions in their draft and then set about eliminating 50 percent of them. They should then consider whether editing out such words eliminated wordiness and improved clarity or perhaps made things worse.
- Ed, of course, should use a spell checker; he could be encouraged to use a grammar checker on occasion, particularly if support is available through the college writing center.
- Ed and his classmates could edit their writing for publication. Issues of editing, agreements and disagreements that heighten the importance of editing, become more visible when writers publish their writing for audiences beyond the classroom.

❑ PROOFREADING

Following the editing process, proofreading is usually the final step before submitting an essay for evaluation or for publication. Proofreading seeks to eliminate typographical and other errors that have not been noticed before. Writers can be assisted in proofreading their own and others' writing.

- Ed and his classmates could proofread one another's essays.
- Ed could ask someone else (a roommate, a spouse, a friend) to proofread his essay.
- Ed could practice some tips for effective proofreading before he submits his final draft for evaluation: read with fresh eyes after letting the draft sit awhile, use a ruler on each line for focus, double-check names, dates, page numbers, and, if time allows, read the essay backward.
- Ed could proofread during class the day the final draft is due. If he catches numerous errors (and marks them in pencil), he knows that he did not proofread carefully enough, or with fresh enough eyes, before bringing his essay to class.

❑ PUBLICATION

In some cases, publication is the desired goal for writing, whether published in-house like some company reports, published commercially like trade books, published academically in scholarly periodicals, or published online at the class or the student's website, on a course management system, or on some other more public venue. Ed can be introduced to aspects of the document design and production process.

- Ed and his classmates could use desktop publishing to produce an edition of their poems on artificial intelligence and distribute it to friends and relatives. At a joint poetry reading, they could exchange copies with a local high school class that has also published an anthology of its poetry.
- Ed could produce a print or digital portfolio of his most significant writing in college, in which the final draft of his essay on AI might be one piece. He could prepare this portfolio for inspection by prospective employers and others.
- Ed could put a cogent cover letter on his essay and mail it to appropriate readers, such as his elected representatives.
- Ed and his classmates could produce a collection of essays for their own knowledge and enjoyment. The teacher could decide to include questions on a final exam that came from this collection of readings as well as from the textbook.
- Ed could publish a document for a specific audience describing his research—a fact sheet on robotics for new students who will enroll in this course the next term or a pamphlet on computers' impact on the

workplace for high school students in a vocational education class. In such cases, Ed would have to consider alternatives in the document design, production, and distribution process.

- Ed could submit his essay for publication to a newspaper or periodical.

Obviously, I am not suggesting that a teacher include all of these suggestions in one course, or even include one element from each of the six stages. Some teachers might want to emphasize the planning process, others the revising process, and yet others some combination of classroom strategies. Likewise, some teachers prefer to give several brief writing assignments rather than one or two lengthy projects that go through several drafts. My goal in each case is to give teachers suggestions for helping students become more effective communicators about the subjects they are studying. The goal for WAC teachers is to move from the traditional paradigm of assigning writing and then grading it to one that develops students' thinking and writing abilities (not just evaluates them) and that envisions students' writing as central to the knowledge being generated by the course.

Focused Oral and Written Conversation about Academic Writing

On pages 26-30, I described letter writing between pairs of students in my Victorian Literature class to enhance their learning of course material and to familiarize them with disciplinary inquiry and conversation. I mentioned there that my students' informal letters were frequently more informed and insightful than their formal essays, and that "I need to improve the way I design and use such essays in my classes" (30). Several iterations later, I think I've discovered one strategy for generating more interesting and insightful results from students assigned to write formal, critical essays. This strategy, like many in this book, combines "writing to learn" with "writing to communicate" to increase students' knowledge of disciplinary subject matter and to improve their effectiveness as academic communicators. When assigning critical essays, I now emphasize the collaborative process for constructing knowledge and communicating effectively about Victorian literature (or other subjects). Students write drafts of essays; they write letters to each other in groups of three or four; and they orally discuss these letters and drafts before and after submitting a final draft. My goal is to help students, who are novices in the discipline, produce informed and persuasive writing in a professional context with publication as a goal. After all, becoming a professional in any discipline means eventually to engage experts in the ongoing conversation of that discipline.

Let me provide you with more specifics on this process followed by a sample "assignment sheet." In this example, students write letters to two or three other students about their critical essays. Without much prompting from me, students correspond about the five conceptual frameworks identified by Anne Beaufort as central to learning and transferring writing and communication skills to new contexts: subject area knowledge, genre knowledge, writing process knowledge, discourse community knowledge, and rhetorical knowledge (*Writing in the Real World: Making the Transition from School to Work,* Teachers College Press, 1999). So that these writers will learn

61

the demands of such knowledge on successful professionals and on their public, academic writing, students are required to respond honestly and holistically and to focus in their letters on the integration of source material into their original thesis or perspective, a continuing problem area for many students. Each student has self selected a different topic about Victorian literature for their critical essay, so the letters they write also focus on subject matter knowledge, as in the following interchange about the poetry of Robert Browning. Huong's first letter, which she brings to class that day as a cover sheet with a draft of her critical essay, reads in part:

> Dear Lauren, Kim, and Professor Young,
>
> It was really hard to come up with the topic for this research paper but ... I found a question worth digging into. I ... decided that what bothered me the most was Robert Langbaum's article on Robert Browning's dramatic monologues. Langbaum claimed that Browning was able to cause readers to feel sympathy for the [poem's] speakers even though they have committed atrocious acts of murder. Before I read "My Last Duchess" and "Porphyria's Lover," I did give this acclamation the benefit of the doubt. However after reading these two poems, I was outraged by the actions of the male speakers. I tried hard to feel sympathy for them but my moral judgment remained strong so I had to dismiss Langbaum's claim. This research paper analyzed two opposing views between moral judgment and sympathy of Browning's dramatic monologues. I tried to find an opposing view to Langbaum and found a really good article written by Melissa Gregory.
>
> I would really like your input on my paper because this is solely based on instinct and my own moral judgments. I will accept arguments and suggestions because I am a firm believer that there are always two sides of an argument. Also look out for grammatical mistakes, spelling, sentence structure, and word choice. I hope you guys enjoy my attempt to straighten out the one complex [issue] that I had with Robert Browning.
>
> Sincerely,
>
> Huong

Huong's letter to her two group members, Kim and Lauren, accompanies a good draft of her essay. Huong explains to us her purpose, her rhetorical strategies, the research question she is attempting to answer, and her worries about correct academic conventions and usage. I believe, as you can undoubtedly tell by now, that this exercise in "writing about your writing" to a responsive audience is valuable in itself, but, maybe even more important, Huong is inviting us to respond to her, to be knowledgeable readers of her prose in process, and thereby to help her become a more effective communicator. This letter of invitation to respond is different from the usual approach in which students receive a critical response from teacher and peers that touches everything these readers choose to comment on, whether or not the writer sees these responses as germane to her purpose. Thus, by benefit of this letter, Huong invites readers to focus on areas of concern to her, rather than issues of concern to them, and she retains some control of this enterprise in academic collaboration. Huong sets the agenda for this discussion. In this class, students in groups of three meet to read each others' draft essays, silently or aloud depending on time, and for each author to read aloud her letter to peers, and then to have an oral discussion of the essay draft in the context of the author's letter. Huong herself has written letters of response to both Kim and Lauren, so they need to share the allotted class time or make arrangements to talk or email after class. The next class period, Huong receives a significant letter of response from both Kim and Lauren, as well as their editorial comments on the manuscript itself and a brief note from me. Here is part of Lauren's response to Huong:

Dear Huong:

I enjoyed reading your cover letter and essay. I liked how you discussed in your cover letter how your reaction to Langbaum's piece sparked your inquiry into this paper....

Throughout the paper, I have few suggestions for syntax, organization of sentences within the paragraphs, and ideas to expound upon (see annotations on text—but I have focused them on the middle/end). After you pose your questions on page five with regard to Langbaum and Dupras's interpretation, I think a stronger transition is needed to contrast them to Gregory's analysis. Breaking up the long paragraph (on page five) and focusing on more in-depth analysis of this juxtaposition of ideas might help the structure.

You cite Gregory's interpretation of sexual violence, but emphasis of this theory is discussed in conjunction with "Prophyria's Lover." Maybe you could include more analysis/synthesis on "My Last Duchess" as well. This would better illustrate Gregory's argument of the "masculine violence ... in the struggle for sexual dominance."

Also, you might want to include more textual analysis of the two works. You could cite several more passages or short phrases from these two poems that parallel with the assertions Langbaum and Gregory cite. Also, the ending of the paper is a little confusing. You only cite "Prophyria's Lover" and not the integration of the two Browning works. Could you find a way to incorporate both in the concluding paragraph? I think this would enhance the thesis and questions initially asserted/posed. Additionally, I would re-work several sentences/ideas in the conclusion for a more powerful interplay with the initial questions. I really like your concluding question; I think it is a powerful idea to grapple with in understanding women's duality and the role of the poetess.

Please let me know if you have any questions about my suggestions or questions on the paper.

Sincerely,

Lauren

Lauren's response to Huong directly addresses issues raised by Huong in the first letter—issues related to interpreting Robert Browning's two referenced poems, to Huong's struggle for understanding and clarification, to the integration of secondary sources, to usage conventions, and to composing a successful academic argument. The reading of the disciplinary research, in this case the literary critic Robert Langbaum, is central to Huong's contribution to scholarly knowledge about Browning's poetry. Huong receives two such thoughtful written responses and manuscript annotations from peers, a brief written response from me, and a further brief opportunity for oral discussion with her readers in class. In addition, she has our email addresses if she has further questions or wants an ear familiar with her manuscript as she is revising.

Huong then revises her critical essay and turns in the final draft soon after. She makes copies (or posts them online) for her group members and writes a final cover letter thanking her responders. She also describes how she has revised the manuscript in response to their suggestions or in response to further thought and research. This process encourages the entire class to assume that every essay, unless it is publishable in its present form, can be further revised and strengthened. Essays by undergraduate students such as Huong aren't expected to be publishable, but I do expect these writers to revise their essays, within the class's time schedule, in order to improve them. I also request that in their final letter, they describe what they believe to be fruitful areas for further research on their topic that might be conducted at a later time. I believe essays written under these classroom conditions are, on average, more clear and insightful than ones written before I began assigning these accompanying letters.

Here is a part of Huong's final cover letter addressed to Kim, Lauren, and me:

> I wanted to thank you guys for taking the time to read my essay and giving me insightful suggestions on how to improve my paper. ... Lauren's suggestion about including more textual analysis of the two works really helped me flush out ideas to backup my outside sources. I did this many times especially in the last couple of paragraphs where she suggested that I needed more integration of the two Browning works. I also found it helpful that Lauren mentioned how I did not include "My Last Duchess" to defend Gregory's theory on sexual violence in Browning's dramatic monologues. I added a new paragraph dedicated to just that; and I think it helped to make my argument stronger....
>
> Kim gave me a new way of looking at how Gregory's point of view was defending women against the male villains; yet ironically she herself was a woman. However, Langbaum's point of view does not include those from a female perspective. It is funny that Kim and I are taking this from a feminist perspective and are defending our rights as non-submissive women. We feel strongly about Browning's subject matter and like Gregory, we have let our emotions and moral judgment hinder our way of thinking.
>
> ... If I had more time and this assignment was longer, it would have been interesting to find more sources perhaps written by a female critic who states our same sentiments. It would also be interesting to do research on how Victorian women felt about Browning's poetry. Or perhaps I would not be able to find such sources because their opinions did not account for much back then. ...
>
> Sincerely,
>
> Huong

In this letter, Huong shows appreciation for the effort of her peers on her behalf, but she also shows her own continued thinking about her argument, about the possibilities of future research, both primary and secondary sources, and about ways she can make a disciplinary contribution to the ways literary critics think about Robert Browning's dramatic monologues.

Huong is writing personally, academically, and conversationally in these letters as a way to consciously reflect on what she is learning and how this learning might be represented and communicated to others. Writing assignments that encourage such metacognitive thinking provide students with frameworks to scaffold their knowledge and experience as they move from class to class across the curriculum and as they prepare for future academic research, disciplinary problems, and communicative tasks, whether in literary criticism, electrical engineering (see pages 21-27), or other disciplines. Below is a sample assignment I hand out to students.

Sample Assignment: Critical Essay with Accompanying Letters

Dear Classmates,

Insert Date: Near final draft of your critical essay with cover letter is due. Bring to class 4 copies (one for each group member, one for me, one for you).

In the essay you should analyze and synthesize one or more works we have studied and contextualize it/them with reference to other writers from our readings of Victorian literature. Your audience is your classmates, me, and the rest of the English department faculty (who will read some of them as part of our departmental assessment). You will work on these essays in groups of three.

Cover Letter: Your essay needs to be accompanied by a cover letter of at least 250 words, single-spaced, addressed to your group members and me in which you tell us: what you are up to, how it is going, what your research question is, what your thesis is, what you think is strong or going well, where you would like our advice, etc. Particularly important: State what advice, feedback, or help would be particularly helpful to you! Staple this cover letter to the front of your critical essay.

Provide a scholarly context for your discussion. Your goal in reading and integrating these secondary sources is to enter the ongoing conversation about the way scholars experience and interpret Victorian literature.

Insert Date: Read and study carefully the draft essays and cover letters of two classmates and then provide them with a significant written response. In addition to making comments directly on the manuscript draft itself, you will write a 400-500 word letter to each author with an extra copy of each letter for me.

You will read two essays and provide substantial feedback to their authors (and they to you about your essay). The purpose of this exercise is to give you the opportunity to write an excellent interpretive essay, an important ability in undergraduate and graduate school, law school, many professions, many places of employment (such as writing grant proposals), and for many citizens participating in a democracy. This assignment will also give you the opportunity to develop your critical reading and editing skills, also an important ability in many work settings—that is, the ability to critique a draft that a colleague has written, to edit a company report, or to collaborate with others in the writing of an important document.

Here are some general guidelines for the process:

- Read the cover letter first to get a sense of what the author says about his or her research questions, thesis, purpose, and organization, and about what she sees as strong and focused in her essay and where she would like some help.
- With the cover letter in mind, carefully read the essay through without making any marks.
- Read the essay through a second time, this time pausing to make comments in the margins (both positive responses and suggestions for revisions, questions, and alternatives). During this process, you are having a dialogue with the author and his text. Your goal as the responder is to help the author in writing an even stronger, clearer, and more insightful and persuasive essay.
- As you read and comment, ask yourself questions: Am I convinced by this claim? Do I need more evidence here? Maybe the writer could refer to Tennyson and Carlyle at this point? Is this point clear? Would more research help here? Is this the right organization—maybe this point ought to come before the earlier point? On page three is a key component of the thesis—should it be moved closer to the beginning? Are there ideas or authors or references that might be useful that the author has not included? And always, with all comments, remember as well to help the writer with the specific areas they requested in their cover letter.
- Read the essay through a third time, this time making editorial comments on spelling, grammar, sentence structure, clarity, repetition, etc. Writers might well appreciate your catching a fragment or suggesting how to make a sentence parallel. On the other hand, this essay will be revised, and therefore that sentence you "correct" might not even be in the next version, so finding "errors" for the author is not the main part of the exercise at this juncture. Again, your main purpose is to be helpful, to give suggestions that will assist the writer in producing a better final draft.
- After you have commented directly on the essay, you will be thoroughly familiar with it. Now write a letter to the author. Your letter should be supportive, honest, and helpful. Tell the writer what you liked about the essay—where it provided you with new insight. Answer or give responses to issues they raised in their cover letters—or provide alternatives. Tell them what interested you the most, where you would like to see more information, what new research might be helpful to their purpose and their argument. Tell them where they have been needlessly redundant and where they may have wandered too far off topic. Suggest ways the essay might be more creative, lively, engaging to read. Again, you are in conversations with the authors— you are not their bosses or their editors—rather you are their colleagues and collaborators—so that's the tone you want to establish in your letter. Provide your colleague with your email address and phone number in case they have questions about what you wrote or what else they might do with their essay.

Insert Date: Final draft of your essay with cover letter is due. Bring four copies to class.

In this cover letter of at least 250 words, single-spaced, addressed to your group members and to me, tell us in what ways you revised your thinking and your writing after doing more research and receiving feedback from others. What revisions did you make? Why? What advice was particularly meaningful? Staple this cover letter to the front of your critical essay.

I look forward to reading your essays.

Best wishes,

Art Y.

Grading

I've said little thus far about the assessment and grading of student writing, and indeed even a cursory discussion of such issues is beyond the scope of this booklet. However, since grading is a part of the writing process for most students and teachers, in the sense that the process is not finished until the essay is graded, I'll conclude by giving some advice on the thorny issue of grading students' formal writing.

Teachers as well as students only have a limited amount of time to give to each project. To most effectively critique and grade student writing, spend most of your allotted time giving feedback on a draft, commenting on strengths, and making suggestions for improvement. The writer will then not only read your comments but do something with them when he or she revises. Students are more likely to read your comments as well as to *understand* and *apply* them in the context of revising their prose. Then when you read the final draft, simply put a grade on it and a brief comment. Extensive comments at this point, when no further revision is contemplated, are not nearly as useful as they are earlier in the composing process.

Teachers have difficulty moving from the teacher-as-mentor role to the teacher-as-evaluator role. After they have mentored a student, seen how much progress he or she has made, observed what difficulties he or she has overcome, it is difficult to step back into the role of "objective" evaluator. There are no easy resolutions to the resulting tension teachers sometimes feel when they want to give students an honest evaluation of their writing and yet encourage further growth and learning. What we should not do is eliminate the tension by retreating from our teacher-as-mentor role. The tension we feel may be a healthy thing, reminding us that teaching and learning are more important than grading whether what we taught has been learned (or guessed correctly) within a particular time frame.

Some teachers, in contrast, are exploring ways to deal with this tension in their teaching. For example, teachers who teach the same course sometimes exchange students' final drafts with a colleague and grade those of their colleague. This allows each teacher to mentor his or her own students, to unreservedly help them become the best writers they can be under the teacher's brief tutelage, while sharing the teacher-as-evaluator role with a colleague who can grade their students' writing from a different perspective.

Other teachers are experimenting with a portfolio method of assessment, in which a collection of a student's writing, sometimes including early drafts of assignments, is evaluated and given a single grade. In evaluating portfolios, teachers can document growth in writing ability over time, can see how a writer's strengths and weaknesses change depending on the assignment, and can often provide a more accurate evaluation of writing ability and performance than would occur by averaging a series of individually graded pieces of writing.

If you ask students to submit drafts, do not grade early drafts, only the final one. Grades on intermediate drafts send mixed messages to students. The goal for student writing and indeed all writing, albeit an idealistic one, is to write to communicate and not to get a grade.

Do not split grades, that is, give one grade for content and one grade for "English." This too confuses students. If you give a student an A for electrical engineering and a D for English, are you saying that he or she is an A engineer but a poor English student? Do you mean to imply to students that effective engineering is totally separate from communicating effectively as an engineer? WAC promotes the concept that effective communication is integral and essential to effective engineering (or accounting or nursing) and cannot be so easily isolated as a discrete skill—a skill that is nice to have, but that is not really necessary for success in engineering.

Whenever you have a borderline case in grading an essay or report, say between a B and a C, give the student the benefit of the doubt. All graders are fallible.

■ Chapter 5: Coda

This monograph is meant to provide an introduction to writing across the curriculum for teachers in all disciplines. As such, my focus has been on discussing theories and applications that can be adapted to most academic disciplines and to most levels of education. I have not discussed issues such as the development of a comprehensive WAC program—guidelines for writing intensive courses or the vital role of writing centers—or issues concerned with "writing in the discipline." Writing in the discipline relates to the development of thinking and writing abilities within particular disciplines, ones that deal with perhaps unique cognitive and rhetorical practices, ones that may not be generalizable across disciplines, such as writing proofs in mathematics, patient histories in nursing, or ethnographies in anthropology. Nor have I discussed the vitally important issue of access to technology and to schooling that supports WAC and that makes ECAC possible, an issue that we must continually address if the promise of literate participation in democratic decision making is to be realized for all people in the twenty-first century. There are many obstacles to teachers' working together across disciplines on matters of teaching and learning, but WAC has created an avenue for identifying and in some cases eliminating such obstacles. This booklet is but a small contribution to an ongoing conversation, and I trust we will together find ways to enrich the conversation, both on our individual campuses through workshops and collaborations and through national publications, meetings, and electronic venues.

■ About the Author

Art Young is Robert S. Campbell Chair in Technical Communication, and Professor of English and Professor of Engineering at Clemson University. He is the founder and coordinator of Clemson's Communication-Across-the-Curriculum program. South Carolina Governor Jim Hodges awarded him the "Order of the Palmetto" in August 2000 in recognition of his role in Clemson being selected as TIME magazine's "Public College of the Year for 2001." In March 2002, he received the Exemplar Award from the Conference on College Composition and Communication for outstanding achievement in teaching, research, and service. In December 2004, he was presented with "The Class of 1939 Award for Faculty Excellence" by the faculty of Clemson University. Dr. Young has co-edited several books on communication across the curriculum, including: *Language Connections: Writing and Reading Across the Curriculum* (NCTE, 1982); *Writing Across the Curriculum: Research into Practice* (Boynton/Cook, 1986); *Programs That Work: Models and Methods for Writing Across the Curriculum* (Heinemann Boynton/Cook, 1990); *Programs and Practices: Writing Across the Secondary Curriculum* (Heinemann Boynton/Cook, 1994); and *Electronic Communication Across the Curriculum* (NCTE, 1998). He has served as a consultant on writing across the curriculum, technical communication, and program evaluation to more than seventy colleges in the U.S. and abroad. He resides in Clemson, South Carolina, with Donna Reiss, his colleague and wife.